Getting the basics right

YOUNG
The *Pathfinder* Series

Catching them young (YPF1)
Peter Satchwell & June de Silva   ISBN 1 874016 40 2

Games and fun activities (YPF2)
Cynthia Martin   ISBN 1 874016 41 0

Are you sitting comfortably? (YPF3)
Telling stories to young language learners
Daniel Tierney & Patricia Dobson   ISBN 1 874016 49 6

Keep talking (YPF4)
Teaching in the target language
Peter Satchwell   ISBN 1 874016 73 9

First steps to reading and writing (YPF5)
Christina Skarbek   ISBN 1 902031 01 6

Let's join in! (YPF6)
Rhymes, poems and songs
Cynthia Martin & Catherine Cheater   ISBN 1 902031 09 1

Making the link (YPF7)
Relating languages to other work in the school
Daniel Tierney & Malcolm Hope   ISBN 1 902031 04 0

Grammar is fun (YPF8)
Lydia Biriotti   ISBN 1 902031 24 5

The literacy link (YPF9)
Catherine Cheater & Anne Farren   ISBN 1 902031 41 5

The RESOURCE *file* Series

Changing places (RF1)
Cross-curricular approaches to teaching languages
Kim Brown & Margot Brown   ISBN 1 902031 05 9

Up, up and away! (RF2)
Using classroom language to help learners say what they want to say
Tony Elston   ISBN 1 902031 25 3

Mixed ability teaching in language learning (RF4)
Susan Ainslie & Sue Purcell   ISBN 1 902031 53 9

A modern image: Enhancing the use of the OHP (RF5)
Daniel Tierney & Fay Humphreys   ISBN 1 902031 55 5

Rhythm and rhyme: Developing language in French and German (RF6)
Cynthia Martin   ISBN 1 902031 49 0

CILT Publications are available through good book suppliers or direct from
Central Books, 99 Wallis Rd, London E9 5LN, Tel: 0845 458 9910, Fax: 0845 458 9912

Pathfinder support materials
for language teachers

Getting the basics right

Nouns, gender and adjectives

Lydia Biriotti

Centre for Information
on Language Teaching and Research

Acknowledgements

I would like to thank many people for their help in making this book a reality, including my colleagues at University College School, all the children who have been guinea pigs for the exercises in the book and Pat McLagan at CILT for all her encouragement. I reserve special thanks for my family, particularly my husband Ralph for his support, and my son Maurice for giving me advice on the structure and content of the manuscript.

The author and publisher would also like to thank the following for permission to reproduce copyright materials: p9 'Quelle est la date de ton anniversaire?' from *Un kilo de chansons* by Jasper Kay (Mary Glasgow Publications); p43 'Les bananes' from *Zozo's French party* by Teresa Scibor (Club Tricolore).

First published in 2001
by the Centre for Information on Language Teaching and Research (CILT)
20 Bedfordbury
London
WC2N 4LB

ISBN 1 902031 40 7

A catalogue record for this book is available from the British Library

Printed in Great Britain by Copyprint (UK) Ltd

Contents

Photocopiable pages

Introduction

Teaching languages effectively has never been more important. Most professionals now agree that starting early and getting children accustomed to language acquisition from a young age is an excellent way of ensuring fluency later on. Many British schools now have French courses for seven to eleven year olds, and a lot of good work has been done to make the language fun and accessible. What many of the new methods have failed to get across is the importance of grammatical rigour in providing a strong platform for accuracy and confidence.

Aims

In *Young Pathfinder 8: Grammar is fun* (CILT, 1998), I argued that grammar and fun need not be antithetical to each other. By taking a structured and creative approach to teaching that combines laughter with logic, extraordinary results can be achieved. The philosophy I outlined can be summarised as follows:

- Insisting on accuracy in the basics is a prerequisite of good language teaching.

- Anything can be taught in an engaging and entertaining manner with enough imagination.

- Far from hampering fluency, as some people argue, an insistence on accuracy can be one of the most useful ways of ensuring a confident and natural approach to speaking and writing.

- Reference to the child's native language is not a barrier to immersion; it simply recognises and uses creatively the fact that for most children the main point of comparison will always be their own native tongue.

- Simply acquiring new words or ideas without a context or framework for understanding and assimilating them is not enough: how new concepts are grouped together is one of the keys to successful teaching.

While *Grammar is fun* was illustrated with several examples of games and activities, it was intended as a methodological introduction rather than a practical resource for teachers in classroom contexts. Since its publication, there has been a great deal of interest in having games and activities available for teachers to use. In response to that demand, this *ResourceFile* takes the principles laid out in *Grammar is fun* and puts them into a format that a teacher can easily put to immediate use with early learners of French.

Getting the basics right takes as its premise the fact that the fundamental pillar on which good language learning is based is the acquisition of basic vocabulary. The easiest place to start is with nouns and the words most closely associated with them, such as articles, adjectives and numbers.

In French, this is a trickier business than most new learners bargain for. For one thing, there is the question of gender, for another the difficult area of agreements. These are the essential building blocks on which mastering the language will rest. Yet so often they are glossed over, or else the difficulties children encounter are not analysed properly. We regularly hear teachers lament the fact that the same basic errors of gender or agreement are still being made by pupils after many years of learning. Perhaps the real error lies not with the pupil or the individual teacher, but with the established methods of teaching gender and agreement.

Approach

The approach taken in this *ResourceFile* is different: it provides a logical and structured approach to understanding these concepts that breaks each problem down into its constituent parts before trying to get children to take it on board. For instance, there is no point asking children to learn the right gender for a noun before they have some way of remembering what the strange concept of inanimate objects having genders is all about!

In each case, the tried and trusted techniques of helping children to engage have been deployed: from story telling to guessing games, from colouring to role-play. But rather than adopting a piecemeal approach to these games, there is a strong structure that underpins the order of the book. Grammar rules are not isolated but aggregated, so that pupils who follow the progression will be building on territory that is increasingly familiar and easy to follow.

The book covers all the building blocks for making sense of French that a child needs before getting a grip on verbs and proper sentences. It focuses on introducing in context the major elements of vocabulary that are required at this stage. But it does so in a way that avoids learning by rote, instead focusing on building appropriate contexts and grammatical building blocks. As such it is intended to form the ideal platform for the early learner in anticipation of tackling complex sentence structure later on.

Structure

The book is divided into four Parts, each with a methodological introduction and some practical notes for the teacher, and then a series of photocopiable worksheets for class use or for independent or group study. The worksheets are designed to be highly motivating and visually stimulating, with easy-to-follow instructions.

- Part 1 introduces basic nouns and adjectives, stressing the importance of getting genders and agreements right from the very beginning.

- Part 2 introduces numbers and definite articles, so that the children can start to develop a sense of singular and plural and to put very basic words together.

- Part 3 develops the theme of agreements by introducing possessive pronouns and adjectival comparison.

- Part 4 covers some prepositions and demonstrative pronouns, providing the key ingredients that children will need as they build up vocabulary before using verbs and making sentences.

Each Part comprises three sections – the first two covering essential grammar and the third offering opportunities to practise what has been learned and to build up new vocabulary. At the end of each Part, a short play offers pupils a chance to relax and enjoy the new grammar and vocabulary in an engaging dialogue. The sequence is not intended as exhaustive. It is imagined that this *ResourceFile* will be used as a companion to other course materials and activities.

The plays have been included as a vehicle for building up an awareness of very basic grammar points and to encourage a flow of dialogue and correct pronunciation. I have exaggerated many regular features so that sentence construction can be easily memorised:

- to assist the children to effect active recall and learn in a passive way patterns of speech and phrases construction;

- to contribute to the liveliness of the play and to give ample opportunity for dramatising the plots by encouraging children to use different voices;

- to help revise grammar points with speed and enjoyment.

This method has already been used with many classes and has led to some wonderful results. The results can be measured by more than just the academic and linguistic achievements of my pupils; they can be measured in the natural way children have taken to the language and the sheer enjoyment that they have derived from the lessons. Used freely and imaginatively, the resources contained in this *ResourceFile* should provide great enjoyment as well as a solid foundation of understanding for all pupils.

Teacher's notes

Contents

Part 1: Nouns and adjectives

Part 1 presents games and exercises specially designed to lay the foundations for confident use of basic vocabulary and grammar. The worksheets will provide the opportunity for children to get off to a good start by focusing on gender and agreements and building up a small working vocabulary and the rudiments of accurate pronunciation.

The activities have been divided into three sections:

- Section A links the acquisition of basic words into an understanding of gender.

- Section B establishes first principles of agreements by taking a gradual approach to the introduction of French rules for adjectives.

- Section C acts as a review of the principles covered and adds further vocabulary to allow children to increase the range of their skills.

Part 1 ends with a simple play, based on a familiar story that exposes children to full sentences and more complex linguistic structures.

Section A

I   *Un jeu de mémoire (p23)*

This deals with the most fundamental issue that confronts native English speakers approaching French: the gender of nouns. Two stories are presented in English – one about a boy, and one about a girl. All the nouns in the boy's story are masculine in French and all those in the girl's story are feminine.

The teacher tells the story in **English**, listing all the nouns in **French** in a column on the board. and pronounces each French word as it is written up.

Pupils are encouraged to pay close attention to the story as it is told and are then asked to repeat the list of English words in the order they appeared in the story, in English. The children are then invited in turn to come to the front of the class and recite the list of objects in English with their back to the board. Each time the pupil successfully names one of the objects in English, the teacher says it in French, exaggerating the sound of the article – *un*. The first to remember all the objects in the story in the correct order wins the game. In this way **children learn the gender of a group of words in English while repeatedly listening to the French word pronounced correctly**. The game can then be repeated with a story about a girl that introduces nouns that are feminine in gender.

When the games have been played, a game of '*Pigeon vole*' is an excellent way of checking that they have understood the exercise. The entire class gives an English word either 'thumbs up' or 'thumbs down' according to whether they think the word was in the story of the girl or the story of the boy.

Only when the teacher is satisfied that pupils have learned to group these specific words together are they asked to memorise the words in French, which they have probably already assimilated by a sort of passive learning in this phase of the exercise.

2   *Prononciation: les objets en classe (p24)*

An exercise using the same vocabulary which requires children to exaggerate the difference in pronunciation between *un* and *une*. This is a good game to play in a group and can be supplemented by pointing at relevant objects and asking '*Qu'est-ce que c'est?*'.

It is crucial to stress the importance of pronunciation – especially the pronunciation of the all-important French article. It is essential to make sure that they make a great distinction between the pronunciation of *un* and *une*. To pronounce *une* you have to purse your lips. To pronounce *un* you just open your mouth in a slightly disgusted fashion! Start therefore by practising these two sounds. The sound 'ane', which is often used as an indeterminate in-between syllable for the unsure is not acceptable! The same attention to detail in pronunciation must later be applied to *le* and *la*.

3   *Dominos (p25)*

The game of dominoes and the memory game that follow provide further practice – children can cut out their own cards and play with a partner under supervision in class.

4   *Les pays et les couleurs (p26)*

Two simple games complete the section, using a simple technique to learn the vocabulary for colours.

The first activity is *une comptine,* a well-known French children's counting game used like 'Eeny meeny miney mo' to determine who will start first. The children stand in a circle. They chant together the rhyme: *'Une automobile ...'*, etc. With each syllable they point in unison to one child after another. When they get to *s'arrêter*, they stop. The child they are pointing at has to name a country from the list, using *en*; you could write the countries on the board. Working through the list they point going round the circle as before, until they get to the named country. This time, the child they are pointing to chooses a colour. The game continues until they reach the chosen colour. The child they are pointing at wins if he/she is wearing something of the same colour.

The second activity is a guessing game in which a child goes out of the room and has to guess the colour chosen by the rest of the class. To come back into the classroom, the child must knock on the door. The class chants *'Qui est-ce?'* to which the child replies, *'C'est moi ... '* (saying his/her name)'. The whole class chants *'Qu'est-ce que tu veux?'*. The child replies *'Une couleur'*. The class asks *'Quelle couleur?'*. The child must choose a colour.

This game can be adapted to guess a fruit, vegetable, animal or indeed any object.

Section B

This introduces adjectives and rules of agreements, building up the rules gradually.

1   *Petit et grand (p27)*

An exercise based on *petit* and *grand,* both of which tend to be used in the same word order as in English, allowing pupils to focus solely on gender without having to worry about unfamiliar sentence structures. This worksheet can be used either in a group context or for individual study.

2   *Rouge et jaune (p28)*

This introduces the concept of adjectives that come after the noun. It uses *rouge* and *jaune*, both of which will be familiar to children from Section A (worksheet 4), and have the advantage of being invariable in the singular.

3   *Vert, noir et bleu (p29)*

This introduces variable colours. Pupils should fill in the colours, using the appropriate adjectival endings. The worksheet is intended for independent study after introduction by the teacher of the activities and notes provided.

4 Le Morpion (p30)

A game of 'Noughts and Crosses' completes this section. Divide the class into four teams. Each member of the first team (*les croix*) plays, in turn against each member of the second team (*les ronds*). The two other teams play against each other in the same way. At the end of the matches, the winning teams play in the final. To put a *croix* or a *rond* on a square, children must create a sentence correctly, without conferring or being prompted, by following the instructions given. The first team that manages to get three noughts or three crosses in a row, wins the game.

Section C

1–4 Les fruits; Les légumes; Que suis-je? and Qu'est-ce que tu veux?

This section opens with self-contained worksheets that can assist in building additional vocabulary in preparation for games in Parts 2 and 3. Draw the children's attention to the fact that all names of fruits and vegetables that don't end with an 'e' are masculine. Most names of fruits and vegetables ending with an 'e' are feminine.

These worksheets are supplemented by some questions and answers. Children should be encouraged to generate their own questions as this is one of the keys to communication.

1 Les fruits (p31)

Ask the children to repeat after you, all the names of the fruit several times in unison. Continually check the pronunciation. Point out to them the fact that all fruits ending with an 'e' are feminine. (Exception is *un pamplemousse.*) All fruits not ending with an 'e' are masculine. (Exception is *une noix de coco.*) The following games can be used to practise the vocabulary before tackling the exercises (see notes below).

a *'Pigeon vole'*: A way of checking if the children have understood how to differentiate between the masculine and feminine words. The teacher reads out a list of nouns without their article. The class gives the French noun the 'thumbs up' or the 'thumbs down' according to whether they think the noun is masculine or feminine.

b *'Kim's Game'*: Ask the children to draw, colour and label in French some cards with one different fruit on each. Make sure they write the fruit with its correct article and spelling. Place all the flashcards face up on the table. Help the children to memorise all the names of the fruits with their colours. One child has to go out of the classroom whilst only one card is removed. The child comes back in and has 30 seconds to work out which flashcard is missing. He or she has to name the missing flashcard (fruit with its respective colour).

c *'Monsieur Tartonpion a ...'*: This game is played along the same lines as 'I went to the market'. Each child holds one flashcard for all to see. One child begins the game by saying *'Monsieur Tartonpion a ...'* and has to name the flashcard he/she is holding (fruit with its respective colour). The next child has to repeat *'Monsieur Tartonpion a ...'* and has to name the flashcard the first child is holding and then add the name of the flashcard he/she is holding. The third repeats everything the second child said and then has to name the flashcard he/she is holding, etc. The game continues with each child repeating what the last child said and naming the flashcard he/she is holding. Anyone who makes a mistake, is out of the game, but must still hold his/her flashcard up for the others to see. The winner is the one who can name correctly all the fruits with their respective colour on all the flashcards. For example:

'Monsieur Tartonpion a une pomme rouge.'

'Monsieur Tartonpion a une pomme rouge et une poire verte.'

'Monsieur Tartonpion a une pomme rouge, une poire verte et un citron jaune.'

'Monsieur Tartonpion a une une pomme rouge, une poire verte, un citron jaune, et une cerise rose', etc.

7

8

Worksheet exercise

To play this game you need to use one different flashcard (with a fruit) for each child plus six cards with a different question and cue answer, on it.

Ask pupils to make six question cards by copying on one side of each card, one question with its cue, from the six questions given in the vocabulary list, and a question mark on the reverse.

Because asking questions, in French, can involve the use of some words that are difficult to read or pronounce ask all the children to repeat after you, the questions with their cue. Pronunciation and intonation are crucial.

Make sure the children understand all the questions and are able to use the cue for the correct answer.

Ask six pupils to stand up and pick up one of the six question cards you have prepared. The rest of the class stays seated and each holds one flashcard (depicting a fruit) for all to see.

The six pupils must walk around the class asking every seated child in turn the question that is on his or her card. The questioner must make sure that the child answering the question uses the right cue and that he/she adds the name of the fruit on his flashcard.

For example, if a pupil holding the flashcard with a 'water melon' is asked:

'Qu'est ce que tu regardes?'. The child has to answer: *'Je regarde une pastèque'*. When another one asks *'Qu'est-ce tu colories'* he/she answers *'Je colorie une pastèque'*, and so on, using all six questions.

In this way every child has to answer correctly six different questions naming the one fruit on his/her flashcard. The game should be repeated with six different children asking the questions.

Role-play is an effective way of building the confidence of new learners and encouraging them to participate, sometimes to the point that they forget they are talking in French. Many less able children can take part and derive pleasure from the knowledge that their contribution is as valuable as the others. They accept to have their pronunciation corrected as they take pride in sounding 'very French'!

Write on the board or OHP a little conversation along these lines:

– *Bonjour, Monsieur/Madame.*   – *Bonjour.*
– *Qu'est-ce que vous désirez?*   – *Je voudrais un/une …*
– *Voilà.*   – *Merci, c'est combien?*
– *C'est … Francs*   – *Oh, là, là! C'est trop cher!*

For props you could use the flashcards you have prepared or better still some plastic fruit and toy French money.

2 Les légumes (p32)

Introduce the vegetable vocabulary and all the activities and games associated with it, in the same way as the fruit vocabulary on worksheet 1.

Draw the pupils' attention to the fact that all names of vegetables that end with an 'e' are feminine. (Exception: *un concombre*). All the names of vegetables that don't end with an 'e' are masculine.

To prepare for all the games and activities ask the children to draw, colour and label in French some cards with one different vegetable on each. Make sure they that they use the correct article and spelling for the vegetables.

3 Que suis-je? (p33)

Introduce the animal vocabulary and all the activities and games associated with it, in the same way as the fruit vocabulary on worksheet 1.

To prepare for all the games and activities ask the children to draw, colour, and label in French some cards with one different animal on each. Make sure they that they write the animal with its correct article and spelling.

4 Qu'est-ce que tu veux? (p34)

This practises questions and adjectival agreements, building on the previous work on gender.

5 Les jours de la semaine. Les mois. Les nombres (p35)

A vocabulary sheet included as preparation for games in Parts 2, 3 and 4. This introduces days of the week, months and basic numbers. This sheet is intended for use in the classroom.

To teach **the months of the year** with a good pronunciation, the following simple chant from *Un kilo de chansons* by Jasper Kay (Mary Glasgow Publications) could be used, said as a rap:

1 Quelle est la date de ton anniversaire?
  Janvier, février, mars. (*bis*)

2 Quelle est la date de ton anniversaire? (*bis*)
  Avril, mai, juin. (*bis*)

3 Quelle est la date de ton anniversaire? (*bis*)
  Juillet, août, septembre. (*bis*)

4 Quelle est la date de ton anniversaire? (*bis*)
  Octobre, novembre, décembre. (*bis*)

As they sing, children should stand up and sit down again when the month they were born in is sung. This is a good exercise for encouraging good pronunciation and active participation in class.

Numbers could be introduced with a game of *'Quelle heure est-il, Monsieur le Loup?'* ('What's the time, Mr Wolf?'). Select one of the children to be the first Monsieur le Loup. The class asks the 'wolf' the question *'Quelle heure est-il, Monsieur le Loup?'*. He must reply with a time of his choosing, such as *'Il est sept heures'*. The class then has to count in unison up to that number (*'Un, deux, trois ...'*). They then ask the time again and the process is repeated. When Monsieur le Loup decides on a mealtime (*'Il est une heure: c'est l'heure du déjeuner'*), everyone must run away from him as fast as possible. If the 'wolf' manages to catch one of them, then the child caught becomes the next Monsieur le Loup.

It can also be very effective to use a ball to enhance the process of memorising numbers. Ask the children to take a ball and bounce it against a wall, and then catch it. They must count in French. How many times can they do this without dropping it? If they let it drop or mispronounce a number, they are out. Get them to count in twos, in fives, in tens. Faster and faster, or even backwards!

To help children remember the obligatory *et* in for instance *vingt et un,* it can help to count out aloud with the whole class. When you all reach 21 or 31, etc the children have to raise their voices and get up as they are saying *'et'* and sit down quickly. Carry on counting. This can be repeated faster and faster!

6 Boucle d'Or et les trois ours (p36)

The play at the end of this section is a simplified French adaptation of *Goldilocks and the three bears* that revises much of the vocabulary and grammar covered so far. This story was chosen because:

■ there are a lot of repetitive sentences to help children to get their tongues around difficult pronunciation. Preparation and memorisation are very important. Continually listening and

9

repeating the dialogues helps pupils to focus and familiarise themselves with very basic sentences construction and promotes passive learning;

■ children love using different voices, so encourage them to do so.

For props, children should bring in three bears of different sizes and a pretty doll. You need a table and three different sized chairs, three bowls and spoons, and three different sized boxes for beds.

To role-play the various parts, the class can be divided into groups of four, each to perform the play. The teacher can act as a narrator, at least to start with, to hold the drama together. At first, each group can read out the script, but they should be encouraged to memorise some parts and become more fluent and more convincing each time they perform. Make sure the children use the right pronunciation and the right intonation. Teachers should insist on children emphasising key words such as *grande* or *petite*.

Part 2: Numbers and articles

Part 1 concentrated on establishing a basic vocabulary and introducing the notion of gender. The games and exercises in Part 2 are designed to build on these skills and develop pupils' understanding of the definite article and the construction of plurals.

- Section A introduces the definite article and its various forms in the singular.

- Section B introduces plurals by linking numbers and agreement together in a series of fun games.

- Section C provides exercises which practise the definite article and plurals, as well as introducing further vocabulary.

Finally a play is presented that will begin to stretch children's knowledge and understanding of these simple ideas, so that by the end of the unit, all those who have followed the exercises will be confident and fluent in plural usage.

Section A

This section introduces the definite article and builds on the previous work on agreements.

1 Le, la ou l' (p38)

A simple activity that allows children to use familiar vocabulary (relating to animals) and simply place *le*, *la* or *l'* before the appropriate word. This is a straightforward exercise, but one that many course books omit, with the result that the issue of which definite article to use can be over-mystified. The consequences of this for later learning can be disastrous.

2 Le labyrinthe: les fruits (p39)

A linking activity. Learning to link nouns of the same gender with coloured lines should be a familiar technique, and if the teacher stresses the definite article in each case, the consolidating effects of the activity will be significant.

Teachers can further reinforce this by repeating the exercise as provided with familiar objects instead of fruits. Teachers should remember to use every opportunity to remind children of the importance of correct pronunciation.

3 Les transports (p40)

This draws a specific distinction between the definite and indefinite articles. Children are asked to colour in a series of objects that are accompanied by the indefinite article (e.g. *une ambulance*). Once they have done so, they become not generic objects but specific examples and the appropriate article to use is definite e.g. *L'ambulance est blanche*. By giving a specific context to the distinction, it is easier to make the point about different articles clearly: children are likely to remember that once an object is coloured, it becomes specific and therefore needs a definite article.

4 Les vêtements (p41)

This reinforces use of the definite article through a conversation in a shop. Specific items need a definite article: wanting **a** shirt is not the same as wanting **the** shirt. The effort of getting these distinctions right in the early stages is easily rewarded. Not only do pupils understand the point being made, but they also learn to think grammatically and to formulate logical distinctions in their minds.

Section B

Now that the definite article has been mastered and children have acquired a logical understanding of agreements, the plural can be introduced.

1   *Il y a combien de? (p42)*

A simple series of questions and answers. The key to this exercise, which also introduces numbers up to ten, is to get children to remember not to pronounce the final 's' of the plural.

2   *Chanson (p43)*

Rhymes and songs can be very useful in stressing the importance of pronunciation, as they are chanted together and children tend to remember the correct pronunciation in order to join in. The song that follows, '*Les bananes*,' is taken from the cassette *Zozo's French Party* by Teresa Scibor (Club Tricolore).

Stress the 'e' at the end of '*bananes*' but don't pronounce the 's'! The song is sung to the tune of '*Frère Jacques*'. Although very simple, it provides a good introduction to the fact that the 's' of the plural noun is silent, as is the 's' of the adjective that qualifies it. At the same time, it also introduces children to the idea that the plural noun is prefixed by the word *les*, which is the plural form of both *le* and *la* and agrees with the noun in the plural.

The song can be further adapted by using a technique that will by now be familiar to the class. Ask the children to colour code the two lists of fruit. The feminine list should be coloured in red and the masculine list in blue. Draw the children's attention to the fact that all the fruits ending in 'e' are feminine. Pupils are asked to write their own song, replacing the noun *banane* with their favourite fruit. Point out the importance of adding an 's' to the fruit and to *bon* or *bonne* in order to form the plural and make the adjective agree. Also explain why '*une pour moi*' changes to '*un pour moi*' if the fruit they have chosen appears in the blue column on the board.

The song can be repeated using any object children may choose.

3   *Le labyrinthe des légumes (p44)*

This uses the same basic colouring rules and helps to increase children's understanding by showing them that adjectival agreements extend to number as well as gender. Teachers should not forget to use the material as an opportunity to practise pronunciation as well as grammar.

4   *Les fruits et les légumes (p45)*

Now that pupils are familiar with number and gender agreements, they are given an opportunity to construct sentences for themselves (such as *livres verts*).

5   *Les animaux: colorie, compte et écris (p46)*

This provides further sentence-building practice, while practising animal vocabulary.

6   *J'adore/je déteste (p47)*

A further activity adds a different twist to the use of plurals. When making general comments such as 'I love rabbits', the French use the definite article: *j'adore les lapins*. Ask the children to complete the sentences using the key provided, and draw their attention to this grammatical difference between French and English.

7   *Des et les (p48)*

This introduces the plural of the indefinite article *des*, as opposed to the definite *les*. Some examples in context for instance might usefully assist children at this stage.

Section C

These activities review and revise the material covered so far. They are intended as enjoyable ways of building up confidence and fluency with material which should by now have been mastered, using two tried and tested approaches: drawing and mime:

I   *La tête et le corps: dessine et colorie (p49)*

A drawing activity (always engrossing for children) draws attention to the French use of the definite article in referring to parts of the body. The opportunity for children to draw a monster seldom fails to entertain. Teachers should ensure that gender and the use of the article are well understood here.

A different entertaining way to introduce the plural with body vocabulary is using miming songs such as *'Savez-vous planter les choux?'*, a well-known old French nursery rhyme.

The music for this song can be heard on the website *Sommaire des chansons* (http://ourworld.compuserve.com/homepages/Thierry_Klein/sommaire.htm) or follow the link from the on-line resources page of NACELL (www.nacell.org.uk).

Children hold hands and sing: Each time they mention a different part of the body they mime the action accordingly. As you introduce the new vocabulary, draw their attention to the fact that the final 's' and 'x' that mark the plural are silent.

Savez-vous planter les choux, A la mode, à la mode, Savez-vous planter les choux, A la mode de chez nous? On les plante avec les pieds A la mode, à la mode, On les plante avec les pieds, A la mode de chez nous.	*les jambes* *les genoux* *les bras* *les coudes* *les mains* *les doigts* *les oreilles* *les yeux* *les fesses*

Another good way of introducing some additional body vocabulary is by teaching pupils a lively, popular song: *'Alouette'*, following the same process as above.

I   Alouette, gentille alouette,
    Alouette, je te plumerai.
    Je te plumerai le bec, (*bis*)
    Et le bec, et le bec,
    Alouette, alouette, Ah!

2   Je te plumerai les yeux (*bis*)
    Et le bec, et le bec,
    Alouette, alouette, Ah!

3   Je te plumerai la tête (*bis*)
    Et les yeux et les yeux,
    Et le bec, et le bec,
    Alouette, alouette, Ah!

4   Je te plumerai le cou (*bis*)
    Et la tête, et la tête,
    Et les yeux et les yeux,
    Et le bec, et le bec,
    Alouette, alouette, Ah!

5   Je te plumerai les ailes, (*bis*)
    Et le cou, et le cou,
    Et la tête, et la tête,
    Et les yeux et les yeux,
    Et le bec, et le bec,
    Alouette, alouette, Ah!

6   Je te plumerai le dos (*bis*)
    Et les ailes et les ailes,
    Et le cou, et le cou,
    Et la tête, et la tête,
    Et les yeux et les yeux,
    Et le bec, et le bec,
    Alouette, alouette, Ah!

7   Je te plumerai les pattes (*bis*)
    Et le dos, et le dos,
    Et les ailes, et les ailes,
    Et le cou, et le cou,
    Et la tête, et la tête,
    Et les yeux, et les yeux,
    Et les bec, et le bec,
    Alouette, alouette, Ah!

2 *Le jeu de Picasso. La figure (p50)*

A drawing exercise which familiarises children creatively with vocabulary for the face and the routine use of the definite article.

3 *Les portraits (p51)*

Another drawing game mixes the use of the definite and indefinite articles with appropriate adjectives. People are described and children must draw their faces. To begin with, the teacher should invent the descriptions, taking care to include examples of both the definite article (for hair and eyes, e.g. *'Il a les cheveux blonds.'*) and the indefinite article (for anything else, e.g. *'Il a une grande bouche.'*). Once the children get the hang of it, they can make up descriptions for themselves.

4 *Dessine et colorie (p52)*

The idea above is extended to complete portraits with props such as umbrellas and hats.

5 *L'Extra Terrestre (p53)*

Once the idea of drawing a picture according to a description in French has been mastered, a game can be played. Here, a spinning top is made to generate a random set of adjectives and numbers. Based on whatever the top generates, monsters are drawn: creatures with two blue heads, six green eyes, etc. Divide the class into teams; pupils take turns to spin the three tops and each team then draws their monster accordingly and write a description below. The game can be turned into a highly engaging competition, and prizes can be awarded for the best E.T.

6–7 *Les métiers* and *Un jeu de mime (p54 and p55)*

In order to revise the use of gender, a series of miming games has been included. One of the benefits of using them at this stage is that any children who have so far been too shy to participate fully can get involved without having to talk. Once the principle of the mime has been established it can be used to revise a variety of different things: professions and adjectives have been included here, but teachers could invent their own contexts for miming exercises and guessing games. N.B. Remember to tell the children that, in French, no article is used in describing what job you do, e.g. 'I am a teacher': *'Je suis professeur'*.

8 *Poisson d'avril! (p56)*

This play serves as a useful way of practising grammar points raised in Parts 1 and 2. *Poisson d'avril:* 'April fool's day', is widely celebrated in France, with children tying a paper fish on the back of an unsuspecting friend. The story is straightforward and easy to stage, but the role of M. Bertrand needs to be played by the teacher or by a very confident child. The play can be adapted to the size of the class by adding more questions and answers giving the opportunity for every child to participate. The parts need not be memorised, they are just as effective when read out. Teachers should ensure that pronunciation is good and that children genuinely understand what they are reading.

For props you need to draw a fish, on a thick piece of paper about 30 cm long. Cut it out and thread it with a long string. Pin it to the back of M. Bertrand.

Part 3: Possessive pronouns, adjectival comparison and demonstrative pronouns

Part 3 aims to consolidate children's understanding of adjectives and to add three further dimensions to their knowledge: the use of the possessive, the demonstrative adjective ce, and the construction of comparisons and superlatives. It focuses on demonstrating to pupils how easy it is to continue building up further linguistic skills once the basics have been mastered.

Accordingly, Part 3 is shorter than the previous two, and the first two sections are less about introducing new ideas and more about a gradual reinforcement of ideas.

- Section A introduces the possessive adjective *mon*.

- Section B introduces *plus*, *moins* and *aussi*, as well as *ce*.

- Section C does not provide additional revision as in the previous two parts, but revises numbers from the previous part in a new context: time and date.

  The section ends with a play that consolidates all the material that has come before. It has been designed to promote maximum fluency, and, of course, enjoyment!

Section A

Section A introduces possessive adjectives using *mon*. The exercises are specially designed to draw out the importance of agreement.

1   Ma famille (p59)

This familiarises pupils with the use of *mon*, *ma*, and *mes* in the simplest context: the family. Common errors in this context are easy to spot and correct: the child that says *mon sœur*, for instance, can easily see the error once it has been pointed out. Children should be encouraged to use the game for creating imaginary families as well as discussing their own, as this will add further applications of the learning.

2   Mon/ma/mes + les vêtements (p60)

Once children have grasped the principle of making 'my' agree with the gender of people, you can introduce the idea of the word for 'my' agreeing with the gender of other nouns, like clothes. The rule about using *mon* rather than *ma* for a feminine noun that begins with a vowel is also introduced here.

3   Moi! (p61)

As an extension to the drawing games of Part 2, drawing captioned self-portraits helps to remind pupils that possessive adjectives must also follow agreement rules.

It might be useful first to revise the body vocabulary, using the French translation of the well-known song, 'Head, shoulders, knees and toes'. You can find a lovely example of how this done in the *Muzzy* video produced by the BBC. For a more advanced class, try singing it using the possessive adjectives *mon*, *ma*, *mes*!

4 Ma famille (p62)

In order to consolidate the learning about *mon*, the family can also be described more extensively. This activity allows for the seamless introduction of the use of *il* and *elle*, as well as of the formulae *il s'appelle*, *il a ... ans*, etc. These are often the first items to be introduced to new learners of French, however introducing *il* and *elle* in context is much more likely to make sense of them. By the time children approach them in this context, having already mastered the building blocks along the way, they will seem natural and straightforward.

5 Les aliments et les boissons (p63)

Extending *mon* to *ton* is an important next step. This exercise, in the form of a simple quiz, is both entertaining and informative. Teachers should use it to encourage maximum interaction and dialogue. Teachers could ask pupils to exaggerate their emotions in order to encourage consideration of pronunciation and how they express themselves.

6 Mon animal (p64)

A description of a pet (or imaginary pet) allows all the new learning to be consolidated: *mon*, *il s'appelle*, *il est/elle est*.

7 Ma maison (p65)

Similarly, the description of a person's house (or imaginary house) provides many opportunities for building fluency. This is combined with making a cut-out house.

8 Mon/ma/mes: écrivez (p66)

This written exercise provides revision of the mechanics of agreements with *mon/ma/mes*.

Section B

Section B introduces two concepts: comparisons with *plus*, *moins* and *aussi*, and the demonstrative *ce*. Both concepts expand a child's sense of what adjectives can do, in ever more entertaining ways. There is a powerful immediacy about pointing out this object as opposed to that, or saying that such and such a person or pet is smaller/taller/smarter/less pretty than another. Accordingly, the four worksheets have each been designed for maximum engagement and fun. Section B provides an opportunity for children to enjoy their newly discovered sense of grammatical logic and their language acquisition skills.

1 Plus ... que, moins ... que ou aussi ... que 1 (p67)

Pupils tick the boxes if the statement seems true. However, a variant can also be played using the rules from the popular television show *Play your cards right*, and requires a little preparation. Teachers should cut out three large cards and write one of the comparison phrases *plus grande*, *moins grande*, *aussi grande* on each. Then divide the class into teams and use an ordinary pack of playing cards. Each team has to guess whether the next card that is turned over will be higher than, lower than or the same as the previous one by using the correct French card. If the team gets it wrong, advantage is passed to the other team and points are collected along the way.

2 Plus ... que, moins ... que ou aussi ... que 2 (p68)

A written exercise using the same concept, but different words help to reinforce the point.

3 Ce, cet, cette et ces (p69)

The demonstrative adjective *ce* is introduced using a simple circling game that should recall the way in which *mon* was presented earlier. Teachers can complement the exercise by pointing at familiar objects and getting children to identify them with *ce*, *cette* or *ces*, e.g. *ce stylo* or *ce crayon*.

N.B. Remember to tell pupils that in the case of a 'hard h' like the one in *haricots*, you do not pronounce the 's' in *ces*: *ces haricots verts*.

4   Blockbuster (p70)

To reinforce the use of *ce* and have some fun, this game is based on another popular television show, *Blockbusters*. Children work in teams. When a team gets the use of the demonstrative right they can claim one hexagon as their own. One team tries to capture hexagons going across from left to right; the other top to bottom. The first team to capture a consecutive line from beginning to end wins. This game could be played on the OHP, with teams instructing their leaders as to which hexagon to mark.

Section C

Section C presents some simple exercises that teach children to tell the time as well as a play that helps pull together some of the key features of the grammar introduced so far.

1   Quelle heure est-il? 1 (p71)

A simple exercise in telling the time for times on the hour serves as a written introduction to the time in French. The key for teachers is to remember to stress the importance of spelling *heures* with an *s* when the number of hours is more than one.

2   Quelle heure est-il? 2 (p72)

This introduces the concept of minutes past (or to) the hour, also *et demie* and *et quart*.

3   Quelle est la date d'aujourd'hui? (p73)

The expression of the date in French should also be straightforward, but teachers should remember to stress the importance of not using capital letters for the names of months. These written exercises will help to emphasise the point.

N.B. Remember to point out that in the case of the first of the month, *premier* is used, never *un*.

4   Quelle heure est-il ? 3 (p74)

Written practice of telling the time, based on digital clocks. If pupils have their own watch, the teacher could ask them the time at different points in the day.

5   Beau et belle (p75)

This maze game uses the same basic colouring rules seen before, and serves as a way of furthering children's understanding by showing them the demonstrative adjectives in action and the adjectival agreements of *beau* and *belle*. The use of *beaux* allows the introduction of the standard exception to the addition of the plural *s*: the use of *x* for some adjectives. Teachers should not forget to use this as an opportunity to practise pronunciation as well as grammar.

Pupils can also be asked to describe everything they are wearing as 'beautiful' (e.g. *ce beau pantalon gris*) to complete the exercise.

6   La belle au bois dormant (p76)

A play that has many features specially designed to aid revision and fluency. This version of *Sleeping Beauty* has been specially adapted to provide opportunities for children to learn one more grammatical point: the superlative. It should not be difficult to get the hang of given the introduction to comparisons in Section B. Once again, the play can be read out or performed by different teams of children. Emphasis should be placed on pronunciation and fluency.

For props, encourage pupils to make their own *bâton magique* by decorating a ruler or long stick with coloured ribbons and a gold or silver star.

Part 4: Prepositions and basic sentence construction

This *Resource File* aims to help children to achieve confidence and fluency with all the basics of the French language that can be mastered before tackling verbs and full sentences. One of the most important items that fall into this category are prepositions, especially *au* and *du* with all their variants and agreements. Understanding them is fundamental to mastering French; Part 4 focuses on them intensively.

- Section A introduces a range of prepositions and especially *au* in a number of different contexts.

- Section B concentrates on *du* and its variants.

- Section C provides exercises that use both.

The final play, an adaptation of *Little Red Riding Hood*, gives an exaggerated version of the tale that is perfect for giving the prepositions a thorough workout.

Section A

Section A is designed to give an engaging introduction to prepositions, and to lay out the different forms that *au* may appear in.

1 Sur, sous, dans, devant, derrière (p78)

A song arranged to the tune of *'London's burning'* using the major prepositions. Children can sing it and mime relevant movements: one hand remains still while the other moves above, below, behind as appropriate. The song was devised by Christina Skarbek (CILT, 1998) and provides a wonderfully lively introduction to the theme. It has been followed up here with some simple written consolidation exercises.

2 Un jeu de mémoire: en ville (p79)

Some prepositions, such as *à* change according to their context in French. We say *à la fille* but *au garçon*. This concept is complicated for an English-speaking child. Rather than leaping in, this exercise allows two stories to be told that link together words that take *à la* (feminine nouns) and words that will take *au* (masculine nouns). The stories are reminiscent of the method used for introducing gender in Part 1 A Worksheet 1. They are used as the basis for a memory game: once children can remember which places in a town are masculine and which are feminine, it will be much easier for them to apply the correct variable preposition.

4 Rendez-vous I (p80)

The role-play format can be adapted to include any new vocabulary that needs to be practised. Toy telephones (or phones made out of yoghurt pots) are a useful prop for a variety of conversations, particularly for setting up meetings between people. Display the vocabulary provided on the OHP, and set out some key sentences to help the conversation to run smoothly. Once the class is familiar with words to describe days of the week, times and places, they can invent appointments and arrange to meet over the phone, such as in the skeleton conversation provided.

Allô! Allô! C'est le 24 57 32 11?	*Oui.*
Bonjour Monsieur/Madame.	
Monsieur …/Madame … est là?	*Oui, c'est moi. Qui est-ce?*
C'est …	*Oh! Salut, ça va?*
Oui, très bien, merci.	
Tu veux aller … …? (Exemple: au cinéma)	*Oui!*
Exemple: Alors, rendez-vous le mardi	
sept juin au cinéma à trois heures.	

The format remains the same in each example and children will become increasingly familiar with these simple sentences and the answers they require, and will hardly realise they are practising as they take on different roles. If possible, videotape them as they are acting!

This activity is followed by a coded message. The application of this extra level of complexity is not only engrossing for children; it has the additional advantage of making them strive to get things right first time.

4 *Relie les noms aux prépositions (p81)*

Now that the principles of using *au* and its variants have been established, a simple game of linking words to the relevant form of *au* serves to consolidate the learning. Teachers should remind pupils to use *à* before vowels or a silent h.

5 *Rendez-vous 2 (p82)*

Using *à* with the date and time provides the perfect opportunity to build up different uses of the preposition. How far children go in building up a *rendez-vous* (**at** the post office, **at** six o'clock, etc) is at the teacher's discretion, but the possibilities are considerable.

6–7 *Où as-tu mal?* and *Les glaces: quel parfum? (p83 and p84)*

Two more simple exercises in this unit are intended to show the different forms that *au* may appear in. Pupils could mime illnesses in Worksheet 6.

In Worksheet 7, as well as the colouring and labelling exercises, there is a conversation that can be carried out by children in pairs. It might be useful to make up some flashcards of ice creams and their prices to use as visual aids to help the dialogues along.

Section B

Section B focuses on the preposition *du* and its variants. The emphasis is on seamlessly building up a store of different contexts in which the preposition is used.

1 *Les instruments (p85)*

The first exercise is a simple circling game – pupils are asked to join all the musical instruments that take *du*, those that take *de la*, those that take *de l'* and those that take *des*. The use of musical instruments to introduce the theme is in part because of the peculiarity of French compared to English in using a preposition to express *I play the trumpet* at all. But in part it is also because this is very valuable vocabulary and it is good to introduce it in conjunction with this grammatical quirk.

2 *Du, de la, de l' ou des? (p86)*

Similarly, certain types of food are best introduced in the context of this use of *du*. So this exercise presents a range of food and drinks, and children are asked to fill in the blanks with the relevant variant of *du* and to link them accordingly.

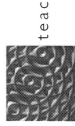

3 **Loto: au restaurant (p87)**

An adaptation of 'Bingo', based on a restaurant menu, further practices the point. Each player needs to choose three starters, main courses, side orders, puddings or drinks from the list given and write them on the grid. All the names of the different foods and drinks are then placed on separate cards in a hat or bag. The game leader then calls out the various dishes, stressing the preposition *du* or *de la*. If a player has the item, he/she puts a cross on the grid and continues to do so until someone completes a grid and wins.

4 **La carte ... (p88)**

A further game of colouring and linking reinforces the point.

Children can be encouraged to make up their own menus using the relevant prepositions as a way of being creative with the prepositions.

Section C

Section C provides opportunities for learning how to use *au* and *du* together. The simple activities should give children the sense that they have genuinely advanced and that using French has become a natural and an entertaining experience.

1 **J'achète ... (p89)**

The first exercise focuses on revising the use of *du* for foods and *au* for locations. The use of the 'Noughts and Crosses' game allows children to work in pairs or groups and build confidence together.

2–3 Les sports 1 & 2 (p90 and p91)

The next exercises focus on the distinction between *faire du* and *jouer au* for sports. Simple linking exercises help to make the point clear. Teachers should reinforce the learning by introducing sports into simple conversations in class e.g. asking pupils what sports they do. Teachers could remind pupils that *jouer au* is used for sports, while *jouer de* is used for musical instruments.

4 **Quel temps fait-il? (p92)**

The introduction to the weather provides more useful basic vocabulary. It also stresses the use of such phrases as *du brouillard* and *du vent*, and links these to phrases such as *à la maison*. Please note that various combinations of weather and activity are possible in the exercise.

5 **Les boissons (p93)**

This worksheet provides practice in using the correct possessive adjective and the preposition *du*.

6 **Le Petit Chaperon Rouge (p94)**

The final play is an adaptation of *Little Red Riding Hood*. It serves as a very lively way of revising much of what has been presented in this. The number of things the mother sends to *Grand-mère* has been exaggerated to create many opportunities to practise the partitive article (*du, de la, des*). Draw pupils' attention to the fact that sometimes the partitive article is expressed by *de* alone, for example, when the adjective qualifying a noun is placed before the noun, as in *'Que tu as de grands yeux,'*, *'de grandes dents'*, etc.

For props the children could make their own little masks or they could use puppets.

The play is ideal for a little exaggerated acting: the perfect way to enjoy recently acquired fluency and confidence in a new language.

Photocopiable worksheets

Contents

un livre

un cahier

un crayon

un stylo

une porte

une montre

une fenêtre

une chaise

une trousse

une gomme

1 Read the boy's story and try to memorise in order all the objects, first in English and then learn them in French.

The little boy's story

It was Jean-Paul's birthday. He received a **book**, an **exercise book**, a **pencil** and a **pen**. He put them all in his new **bag**. He also received a **computer** and a **cassette-recorder**. He balanced the cassette-recorder on top of the computer. It was very heavy. His father told him off. But Jean-Paul could not hear him, as he was listening to his **walkman**.

2 Now read the girl's story and try to memorise in order all the objects, first in English and then learn them in French.

The little girl's story

A little girl opened a door and walked into a classroom. She looked at her **watch**. It was one o'clock. She looked out of a **window**. It was raining. She sat on a **chair**. She opened her **pencil-case**. She took out two things: a **rubber** and a **ruler**. She put them down on **a table**. There were four things on the table: a **calculator**, a **box**, a **television** and a **radio**.

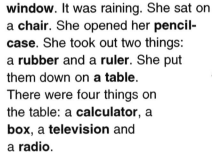

3 Now test your partner on all the French words and their spelling, by pointing to the picture and covering up the label.

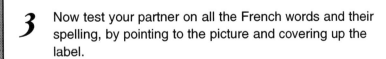

un sac

un ordinateur

un magnétophone

un walkman

une règle

une table

une calculatrice

une boîte

une télévision

une radio

1   Pronounce *un* a bit as if you are disgusted and making an effort: *un … un … un!*

un garçon

un crayon

un stylo

un livre

un cahier

un sac

un ordinateur

un magnétophone

un walkman

2   To pronounce *une* purse your lips: *une … une … une.*

une fille

une porte

une fenêtre

une chaise

une trousse

une gomme

une règle

une table

une boîte

une radio

une calculatrice

une télévision

3   Now take it in turn with your partner to ask what the objects are.

Exemple: Qu'est-ce que c'est?
C'est un crayon.

vocabulaire	**Qu'est-ce que c'est?** = What is this?
	c'est = this is

	un livre		**une calculatrice**
	un ordinateur		**un walkman**
	un magnétophone		**une règle**
	un stylo		**une gomme**
	une boîte		**un sac**
	un crayon		**une table**
	une porte		**une montre**
	une radio		**une fenêtre**

1 Dominos

Découpe les 16 dominos comme ça: [✏ | un livre] et joue aux dominos avec tes camarades.

Exemple: [✏ | un livre | 📖 | un crayon]

2 Un jeu de mémoire

Découpe 32 rectangles comme ça: [🪟] [une porte] Place les cartes en rangs (8 x 4) à l'envers. Chacun à son tour prend deux cartes et les retourne. Il faut trouver des paires – chaque mot avec son image.

Exemple: [🪟] [une fenêtre]

3

Prends les 32 rectangles et colle chaque mot avec son image en deux groupes dans ton cahier: Masculin et Féminin.

Exemple: Masculin

Féminin

1 Une comptine: une automobile

a Une automobile
roule, roule, roule
Où va-t-elle s'arrêter?

– En … *(Nomme un de ces pays.)*
France ǁ Angleterre ǁ Irlande ǁ Ecosse ǁ Belgique
Espagne ǁ Italie ǁ Allemagne ǁ Australie ǁ Amérique

– **De quelle couleur est …?** *(Nomme le pays.)*

(Nomme une de ces couleurs.)
rouge ǁ jaune ǁ mauve ǁ rose ǁ grise ǁ verte ǁ orange ǁ noire ǁ bleue ǁ blanche

– **Avez-vous du … sur vous?** *(Nomme la couleur.)*
rouge ǁ jaune ǁ mauve ǁ rose ǁ gris ǁ vert ǁ orange ǁ noir ǁ bleu ǁ blanc

– Oui.   – Non.
– **Bravo, tu gagnes!** *(On recommence.)*

b Colorie l'automobile en rouge.

c Apprends les noms des couleurs et des pays. Attention à la prononciation!

vocabulaire	**Où?** = Where?
	De quelle couleur est …? = What colour is …?

2 Les couleurs

a Un enfant sort de la classe. La classe choisit une couleur. L'enfant retourne et doit deviner la couleur.

L'enfant tape à la porte: Toc! Toc!
– La classe: **Qui est-ce?**
– L'enfant: C'est *(nom)*
– La classe: **Qu'est-ce que tu veux?**
– L'enfant: Une couleur.
– La classe: **Quelle couleur**?
– *(L'enfant nomme une couleur.)*
– La classe: **Oui, tu gagnes. Bravo! / Non. C'était …** *(La classe nomme la couleur.)*

vocabulaire	**Qui est-ce?** = Who is it? **C'est moi!** = It's me!
	Qu'est-ce que tu veux? = What do you want?
	une couleur = a colour **Quelle couleur?** = What colour?

b Tu peux jouer ce jeu pour deviner le nom d'un objet, d'un fruit, d'un légume ou d'un animal.

un objet: **Quel objet?**	*un légume:* **Quel légume?**	*un fruit:* **Quel fruit?**	*un animal:* **Quel animal?**

un livre

un crayon

un stylo

une porte

une fenêtre

une chaise

une gomme

un sac

un ordinateur

un walkman

une règle

une table

une télévision

une radio

1 Un petit ou une petite + objet?

Nomme chaque objet et dis qu'il est petit.
Ecris: un/une + petit/petite + objet

Exemple: *un petit livre*

_____ _____

_____ _____

_____ _____

_____ _____

_____ _____

_____ _____

2 Un grand ou une grande + objet?

Nomme chaque objet et dis qu'il est grand.
Ecris: un/une + grand/grande + objet

Exemple: *un grand livre*

_____ _____

_____ _____

_____ _____

_____ _____

_____ _____

_____ _____

vocabulaire

petit/petite = small
grand/grande = big

notes

If the noun is feminine, you must
add an 'e' to **grand** or **petit**.

Getting the basics right © CILT 2001. May be photocopied only within the purchasing institution.

un crayon

un stylo

une porte

une fenêtre

une gomme

un sac

un magnétophone

un walkman

une règle

une radio

1   Nomme chaque objet et dis qu'il est rouge.
Ecris: un/une + objet + rouge

Exemple: *une radio rouge*

_____   _____

_____   _____

_____   _____

_____   _____

2   Qu'est-ce que tu regardes?
Ecris: Je regarde + un/une + objet + jaune.

Exemple: *Je regarde une radio jaune.*

_____

_____

_____

_____

_____

_____

_____

_____

_____

_____

vocabulaire	**rouge** = red
	Qu'est-ce que tu regardes? = What are you looking at?
	je regarde = I'm looking at
	jaune = yellow

notes   The order of words in a sentence is not always the same in French as in English. In English, you name the colour first and then the noun you are describing, e.g. a green table. In French, you name the noun first and then the colour: **une table verte** (a table green).

un livre

un sac

1 Vert ou verte?

Exemple: une petite table _verte_   un petit sac _____

un grand stylo _vert_____   une grande chaise _____

une petite porte _____   une petite boîte _____

un grand magnétophone _____   un grand crayon _____

une petite radio _____   un petit livre _____

un grand ordinateur _____   un grand cahier _____

un ordinateur

un crayon

2 Noir ou noire?

Exemple: une petite table _noire_   un petit sac _____

un grand stylo _____   une grande chaise _____

une petite porte _____   une petite boîte _____

un grand magnétophone _____   un grand crayon _____

une petite radio _____   un petit livre _____

un magnétophone

un stylo

3 Bleu ou bleue?

Exemple: une petite table _bleue_   un petit sac _____

un grand stylo _____   une grande chaise _____

une petite porte _____   une petite boîte _____

un grand magnétophone _____   un grand crayon _____

une petite radio _____   un petit cahier _____

une boîte

une porte

un cahier

vocabulaire	**vert/verte** = green **noir/noire** = black **bleu/bleue** = blue

notes	In French, big or small (**grand** or **petit**) is placed before the noun you are describing. If the noun is feminine, you must add an 'e' to _grand_ or _petit_.

The colours **rouge** (red) and **jaune** (yellow) already end with an 'e' so they do not change. You must also add an 'e' to **vert**, **noir** or **bleu** if the noun you are describing is feminine.

une table

une chaise

une radio

1 Joue au Morpion (*'Noughts and Crosses'*). Pour mettre une croix ou un rond dans la case de ton choix dis:

'J'ai + un petit/une petite + objet + blanc/blanche'.
Exemple: J'ai une petite radio blanche.

un livre

2 Ecris: J'ai'+ petit/petite + objet + blanc/blanche.

J'ai une petite chaise blanche.

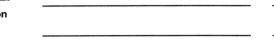
_____   _____
_____   _____
_____   _____
_____   _____
_____   _____

un crayon

un stylo

une porte

un cahier

une chaise

un sac

un ordinateur

un magnétophone

une calculatrice

une télévision

une radio

3 As you increase your vocabulary you can play this game of 'Noughts and Crosses' by forming different sentences. Make up some more sentences starting off with the new vocabulary below.

j'achète = I buy	je veux = I want	c'est = this is

vocabulaire	j'ai = I have	blanc/blanche = white

notes	Blanc does not end with an 'e', so if you are describing something that is feminine, as with **vert**, **noir** and **bleu**, you need to add an 'e' to **blanc**. However, **blance** sounds odd, so an 'h' is added as well: **blanche**.

30

une pomme

une orange

une poire

une banane

une pêche

une cerise

une prune

une pastèque

une framboise

une fraise

une datte

une mangue

un abricot

un melon

un ananas

un kiwi

un citron

vocabulaire

Qu'est-ce que c'est? = What is this?
Qu'est-ce que tu manges? = What are you eating?
Qu'est-ce que tu regardes? = What are you looking at?
Qu'est-ce que tu achètes? = What are you buying?
Qu'est-ce que tu as? = What have you got?

c'est = this is
je mange = I'm eating
je regarde = I'm looking at
j'achète = I'm buying
j'ai = I have

notes

In general, if a fruit ends with an 'e' it is feminine. Exception: **un pamplemousse** (grapefruit). If a fruit does not end with an 'e' it is masculine. Exception: **une noix de coco** (coconut).

1 Les cartes à question: dessine et colorie sur un côté des cartes un grand point d'interrogation et sur l'autre côté copie une question de la liste.

Aprends à prononcer correctement les questions.

?	Qu'est-ce que c'est?

2 Travaille avec ton partenaire. Chacun à son tour pointe sur un fruit et pose une des questions.

Exemple: 'Qu'est-ce que tu manges?'
L'autre répond: 'Je mange un/une …' et il/elle nomme le fruit.

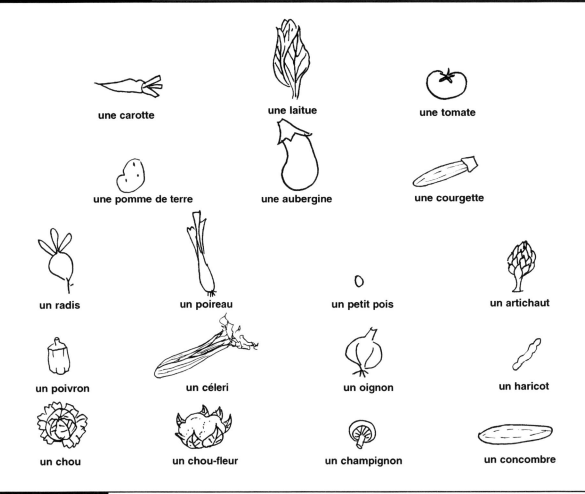

une carotte   une laitue   une tomate

une pomme de terre   une aubergine   une courgette

un radis   un poireau   un petit pois   un artichaut

un poivron   un céleri   un oignon   un haricot

un chou   un chou-fleur   un champignon   un concombre

vocabulaire

Qu'est-ce que c'est? = What is this?	**c'est** = this is
Qu'est-ce que tu veux? = What do you want?	**je veux** = I want
Qu'est-ce que tu manges? = What are you eating?	**je mange** = I'm eating
Qu'est-ce que tu regardes? = What are you looking at?	**je regarde** = I'm looking at
Qu'est-ce que tu achètes? = What are you buying?	**j'achète** = I'm buying
Qu'est-ce que tu as? = What have you got?	**j'ai** = I have

notes

All names of vegetables not ending with an 'e' are masculine.
Most names of vegetables ending with an 'e' are feminine. Exception: **un concombre**.

1   Les flashcartes: prends dix-huit cartes. Dessine et colorie un légume différent sur chaque carte. Ecris 'un' ou 'une' et nomme la légume.

2   Les cartes à question: prends six cartes. Dessine et colorie un grand point d'interrogation sur un côté des cartes et sur l'autre côté copie une question différente.

?	

3   Travaille avec ton partenaire. Chacun à son tour pointe sur une des flashcartes et pose une question.
     Exemple: Qu'est-ce que tu achètes?
     L'autre répond: 'J'achète un/ une …' et il/elle nomme le légume.

1   Colorie les animaux.

Colorie:	1 = rouge	4 = rose	7 = noir
	2 = jaune	5 = vert	8 = blanc
	3 = orange	6 = marron	9 = gris

un chat (7 & 8)

un chien (6)

un cheval (8)

un oiseau (2)

un lion (3)

un perroquet (2 & 5)

un serpent (7)

un poisson (1)

un lapin (8)

un canard (2 & 5)

un cochon (4)

un hamster (6)

une grenouille (5)

une tortue (9)

une souris (8)

2   Mime un animal et demande a ton partenaire: **Que suis-je?**

Le partenaire répond: **Tu es un/une ...**

vocabulaire	**colorie** = colour in	
	Que suis-je? = What am I?	**Tu es un/une ...** = You are a ...

Colorie: 1 = rouge   2 = jaune   3 = orange   4 = vert/e

1   Qu'est-ce que tu veux? Colorie et réponds:
Je veux + un/une petit/e + fruit + couleur du fruit.

Je veux un petit ananas jaune.

Qu'est-ce que tu veux?

_____

_____

2   Qu'est-ce que tu as? Colorie et réponds:
J'ai + un grand/une grande + fruit + couleur du fruit.

J'ai un grand citron jaune.

Qu'est-ce que tu as?

_____

_____

_____

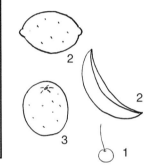

3   Ecris en anglais.

a   Je voudrais une grande banane jaune.   *I would like a big yellow banana.* _____

b   Je veux un grand citron vert.   _____

c   Je voudrais un petit citron jaune.   _____

d   Je mange un petit melon vert.   _____

e   Je voudrais une grande pêche jaune.   _____

f   Je mange un petit abricot orange.   _____

g   J'achète une grande mangue verte.   _____

h   Je colorie un petit kiwi marron.   _____

vocabulaire		
Qu'est-ce que tu veux? = What do you want?	**je veux** = I want	
Qu'est-ce que tu as? = What do you have?	**je mange** = I eat	
je voudrais = I would like	**j'achète** = I buy	
	j'ai = I have	

notes	
	The **j'** of **j'ai** and **j'achète** stands for **je**. The **e** of **je** has been replaced with an apostrophe because '**ai**' and **achète** start with a vowel.

*Si le nom que tu décris est féminin: ajoute **e** à bleu, vert, noir et gris et **he** à blanc.*

Part I C

5 Les jours de la semaine. Les mois. Les nombres

1 Les sept jours de la semaine

lundi ‖ mardi ‖ mercredi ‖ jeudi ‖ vendredi ‖ samedi ‖ dimanche

a Nomme les jours de la semaine en jouant à la balle: lundi, mardi, mercredi … etc.

b Nomme les jours de la semaine à reculons: dimanche, samedi, vendredi … etc.

2 Les douze mois de l'année

Apprends à réciter les douze mois de l'anée. Fais attention à la prononciation!

Est-ce que tu sais les réciter à reculons? Décembre, novembre, octobre …

janvier	avril	juillet	octobre
février	mai	août	novembre
mars	juin	septembre	décembre

3 Les nombres

1 un/une	6 six	11 onze	16 seize
2 deux	7 sept	12 douze	17 dix-sept
3 trois	8 huit	13 treize	18 dix-huit
4 quatre	9 neuf	14 quatorze	19 dix-neuf
5 cinq	10 dix	15 quinze	20 vingt

21 vingt **et** un	26 vingt-six
22 vingt-deux	27 vingt-sept
23 vingt-trois	28 vingt-huit
24 vingt-quatre	29 vingt-neuf
25 vingt-cinq	30 trente

a Joue à la balle en comptant en français. Plus vite! Plus vite!

b Compte deux à deux: deux, quatre, six …

c Est-ce que tu sais compter à reculons? Vingt, dix-neuf, dix-huit …

d Est-ce que tu peux compter jusqu'à quarante (40)? Commence: trente et un (31), trente-deux (32), trente-trois (33) …

Et à cinquante (50)?

vocabulaire	**et** = and	**à reculons** = backwards

notes	Notice that *vingt et un, trente et un,* have *et* instead of a hyphen. All the other numbers from twenty to sixty have a hyphen.

Première partie

Narrateur:	La famille Ours habite dans une petite maison dans la forêt. Voici Papa Ours. Il est gros et grand. Voici Maman Ourse. Elle est de taille moyenne. Voici Bébé ours. Il est tout petit. Il est mignon. Il est adorable! Boucle d'Or est une petite fille. Elle a de longs cheveux blonds. Elle habite dans la forêt. Voici Boucle d'Or. Elle est belle!
	Maman Ourse prépare les céréales pour le déjeuner. Ce très grand bol est à Papa Ours. Ce bol moyen est à Maman Ourse. Ce tout petit bol est à Bébé Ours.
■ *Maman ourse:*	A table Papa Ours! A table Bébé Ours!
Narrateur:	La famille Ours s'assied à table.
▲ *Papa Ours:*	Bon appétit Maman Ourse! Bon appétit Bébé Ours.
Narrateur:	Papa Ours goûte les céréales.
▲ *Papa Ours:*	C'est trop chaud. Allons nous promener en attendant que ça se refroidisse.
Narrateur:	Maman Ourse goûte les céréales.
■ *Maman ourse:*	Oui! Allons nous promener.
Narrateur:	Bébé Ours goûte les céréales.
○ *Bébé Ours:*	C'est très chaud. Youpi! Allons nous promener!
Narrateur:	Les trois ours sortent de la maison. Ils laissent la porte ouverte.

Deuxième partie

Narrateur:	Voici Boucle d'Or. Elle se promène dans la forêt. Elle voit la porte ouverte. Elle est curieuse. Elle entre.
➤ *Boucle d'Or:*	Oh! Quelle jolie maison.
Narrateur:	Elle entre dans la salle à manger. Elle voit la table.
➤ *Boucle d'Or:*	Miam! Miam! Des céréales!
Narrateur:	Elle est gourmande. Elle goûte les céréales du grand bol.
➤ *Boucle d'Or:*	Ooh! C'est trop salé. Ce n'est pas bon!
Narrateur:	Elle goûte les céréales du bol moyen.
➤ *Boucle d'Or:*	Beuh! C'est trop sucré! Ce n'est pas bon!
Narrateur:	Elle goûte les céréales du petit bol.
➤ *Boucle d'Or:*	Miam, miam! C'est bon! C'est délicieux!
Narrateur:	Elle mange toutes les céréales! Elle s'assied sur la grande chaise.
➤ *Boucle d'Or:*	Cette chaise est trop haute!
Narrateur:	Elle s'assied sur la chaise moyenne.
➤ *Boucle d'Or:*	Cette chaise est trop dure!
Narrateur:	Elle s'assied sur la petite chaise.

➤ *Boucle d'Or:*   Cette chaise est très confortable. Oh, je tombe! Oh! là! là!

Narrateur: Elle tombe. La chaise se casse.

Troisième partie

Narrateur: Boucle d'Or monte l'escalier. Elle est curieuse. Elle entre dans la chambre. Elle voit trois lits. Un grand lit. Un lit moyen. Un tout petit lit.

Narrateur: Elle essaie le grand lit.

➤ *Boucle d'Or:*   Ce lit est trop dur!

Narrateur: Elle essaie le lit moyen.

➤ *Boucle d'Or:*   Ce lit est trop mou!

Narrateur: Elle essaie le petit lit.

➤ *Boucle d'Or:*   Ce lit est très confortable. Je suis fatiguée.

Narrateur: Elle s'endort.

Quatrième partie

Narrateur: Les trois ours retournent de la promenade. Papa Ours regarde le grand bol.

▲ *Papa Ours:*   Quelqu'un a goûté mes céréales.

Narrateur: Maman Ourse regarde le bol moyen.

■ *Maman Ourse:*   Quelqu'un a goûté mes céréales.

Narrateur: Bébé Ours regarde le petit bol. Il pleure.

○ *Bébé Ours:*   Quelqu'un a mangé mes céréales. Où sont mes céréales? J'ai faim!

Narrateur: Papa Ours regarde la grande chaise.

▲ *Papa Ours:*   Quelqu'un s'est assis sur ma chaise.

Narrateur: Maman Ourse regarde la chaise moyenne.

■ *Maman Ourse:*   Quelqu'un s'est assis sur ma chaise.

Narrateur: Bébé Ours regarde la petite chaise cassée et pleure.

○ *Bébé Ours:*   Quelqu'un s'est assis sur ma chaise. Et elle est cassée.

Cinquième partie

Narrateur: Papa Ours, Maman Ourse et Bébé Ours montent l'escalier. Ils entrent dans la chambre. Papa Ours regarde le grand lit.

▲ *Papa Ours:*   Quelqu'un s'est couché sur mon lit.

Narrateur: Maman Ourse regarde le lit moyen.

■ *Maman Ourse:*   Quelqu'un s'est couché sur mon lit.

Narrateur: Bébé Ours regarde le petit lit et crie.

○ *Bébé Ours:*   Quelqu'un s'est couché sur mon lit. Regarde Papa, c'est une fille. Elle dort!

Narrateur: Boucle d'Or se réveille. Elle voit les trois ours. Elle saute du lit et court. Les trois ours courent après elle. C'est trop tard!

Getting the basics right © CILT 2001. May be photocopied only within the purchasing institution.

Part 2 A | Le, la ou l'

1 Ecris **le** en bleu avant un nom masculin qui ne commence pas par **a, e, i, o, u** ou **h muet**.

2 Ecris **la** en rouge avant un nom féminin (*) qui ne commence pas par **a, e, i, o, u** ou **h muet**.

3 Ecris **l'** en vert avant un nom masculin qui commence par **a, e, i, o, u** ou **h muet**.

4 Ecris **l'** en orange avant un nom féminin (*) qui commence par **a, e, i, o, u** ou **h muet**.

le chat

la poule*

___ serpent

*l'*oiseau

___ cheval

___ vache*

___ loup

___ âne

___ cochon

___ dinosaure

___ écureuil

___ singe

___ lion

___ ours

___ perroquet

___ tigre

___ lapin

___ grenouille*

___ chien

___ canard

___ phasme

___ souris*

___ tortue*

___ hamster

___ araignée*

vocabulaire	**le/la** = the

Attention! * = nom féminin

38

1   Colorie les fruits:

1 la pomme rouge	7 la prune violette	13 l'ananas jaune
2 la pastèque verte	8 la pêche orange	14 le citron vert
3 la poire jaune	9 la banane jaune	15 le melon jaune
4 la fraise rouge	10 l'orange orange	16 le kiwi marron
5 la mangue orange	11 le raisin vert	17 l'abricot orange
6 la cerise rouge	12 la framboise rouge	

2   Relie les fruits de1 à 12 avec une ligne rouge et de 13 à 18 avec une ligne bleue. Attention! Les lignes rouges et bleues ne doivent pas croiser les fruits ou les lignes noires.

notes	
l' avant **a,e,i,o,u** et **h muet**	**la** avant un nom fémimin
le avant un nom masculin	

Si le nom est féminin, on ajoute **e** à bleu, vert, noir et gris et **he** à blanc.

Getting the basics right © CILT 2001. May be photocopied only within the purchasing institution.

39

1 Colorie les différents modes de transport: 1 rouge 2 jaune 3 orange 4 bleu 5 vert 6 gris
7 noir 8 blanc

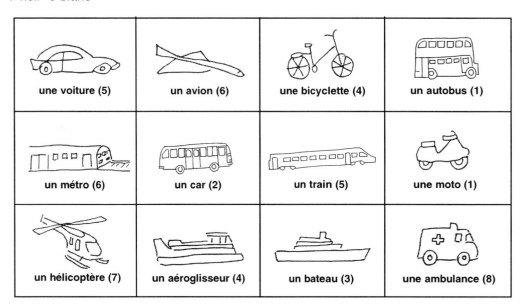

une voiture (5)	un avion (6)	une bicyclette (4)	un autobus (1)
un métro (6)	un car (2)	un train (5)	une moto (1)
un hélicoptère (7)	un aéroglisseur (4)	un bateau (3)	une ambulance (8)

2 **le, l' ou la?**

la voiture ___   avion ___   bicyclette ___   autobus ___

___ métro ___   car ___   train ___   moto ___

___ hélicoptère   aéroglisseur ___   bateau ___   ambulance ___

3 **Réponds aux questions.**

Exemple: De quelle couleur est la bicyclette? *La bicyclette est bleue.* ___

De quelle couleur est l'aéroglisseur? ___

De quelle couleur est l'autobus? ___

De quelle couleur est le train? ___

De quelle couleur est la voiture? ___

De quelle couleur est l'avion? ___

De quelle couleur est le bateau? ___

De quelle couleur est la moto? ___

De quelle couleur est l'ambulance? ___

notes   Si le nom est féminin, on ajoute **e** à bleu, vert, noir et gris et **he** à blanc.

1 Colorie les vêtements: 1 rouge 2 jaune 3 orange 4 bleu 5 vert 6 gris 7 noir 8 blanc

le short (2)

le jean (5)

le pantalon (6)

le costume (5)

le T-shirt (1)

le pull (7)

l'anorak (4)

le sweatshirt (8)

la jupe (3)

la robe (2)

la veste (5)

la chemise (9)

2 **Conversation à la boutique**

Joue avec ton partenaire. Vous êtes à la boutique. Chacun à son tour achète des vêtements. Montre du doigt les vêtements pour les choisir. Le vendeur/la vendeuse invente les prix qu'il/qu'elle veut!

Bonjour, Monsieur/Madame/Mademoiselle.	Good morning, Sir/Madam/Miss.
Je voudrais le/la/l'_____ .	I would like the _____ .
Voilà.	Here you are.
C'est combien?	How much is it?
C'est _____ francs.	It is _____ francs.
Merci.	Thank you.
Au revoir.	Goodbye.

vocabulaire		
10 = dix	50 = cinquante	300 = trois cents
20 = vingt	60 = soixante	400 = quatre cents
30 = trente	100 = cent	500 = cinq cents
40 = quarante	200 = deux cent	600 = six cents

notes

In English we refer to shorts, jeans and trousers in the plural. In French we refer to them in the singular: **le short, le jean, le pantalon.**

Il y a combien de crayons?	Il y a combien de stylos?	Il y a combien de règles?
Il y a six crayons		
Il y a combien de T-shirts?	Il y a combien de chaussettes?	Il y a combien de chemises?
Il y a combien de poires?	Il y a combien de pommes?	Il y a combien d'ananas?
Il y a combien de cerises?	Il y a combien de pêches?	Il y a combien d'oranges?
Il y a combien de carottes?	Il y a combien de pommes de terre?	Il y a combien de petits pois?
Il y a combien de chats?	Il y a combien de canards?	Il y a combien de serpents?

un   deux   trois   quatre   cinq   six   sept   huit   neuf   dix

notes   In general, to make a noun plural add a silent **s** to the noun.

1 Les bananes

Chante cette chanson sur l'air de 'Frère Jacques'.

Les bananes
Les bananes
J'adore ça!
J'adore ça!
Les bananes sont bonnes
Les bananes sont bonnes
Un, deux, trois
Une pour moi!

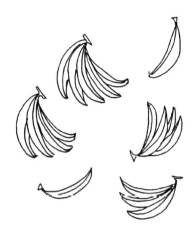

2

Colorie cette case en rose.

la pomme
la banane
l'orange
la poire
la fraise
la prune
la cerise
la datte
la mangue
la mandarine
la figue
la pêche
la pastèque
bonne
une pour moi

Colorie cette case en bleu.

le citron
le melon
l'abricot
le kiwi
l'ananas
bon
un pour moi

3

Adapte cette chanson. Echange 'les bananes' pour le nom de ton fruit préféré.

Mets le nom du fruit au pluriel. Ajoute un **s muet** au nom et à 'bon' ou 'bonne'.

notes

Les bananes *sont bonnes* = The bananas *are good* (taste nice).

Bonnes is used when the noun you are describing is feminine plural.

Bons is used when the noun you are describing is masculine plural.

1 Colorie les légumes.

1 les petits pois verts	8 les épinards verts	15 la menthe verte
2 le chou-fleur blanc	9 le persil vert	16 la carotte orange
3 le chou vert	10 le poivron rouge	17 l'aubergine noire
4 les radis roses	11 les artichauts verts	18 les tomates rouges
5 le poireau vert	12 les champignons gris	19 les pommes de terre beiges
6 le concombre vert	13 le navet jaune	20 les courgettes vertes
7 le céleri vert	14 le maïs jaune	

2 Relie les légumes de 1 à 14 avec une ligne bleue et de 15 à 20 avec une ligne rouge.
Attention: les lignes rouges et bleues ne doivent pas croiser les lignes noires.

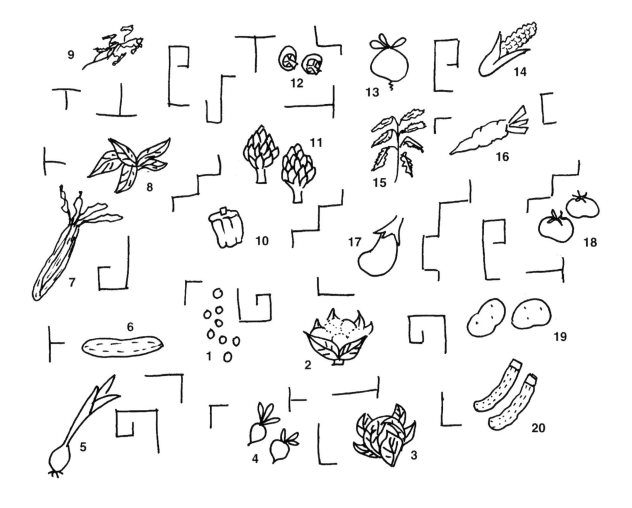

notes	En genéral, pour mettre un nom ou un adjectif au pluriel on ajoute un 's' **muet** au nom. Le pluriel de **le/l'/la** est **les**.

4 Les fruits et les légumes

1 Colorie les fruits et les légumes.

les bananes jaunes   l'ananas jaune   les fraises rouges

les pommes rouges   les poires vertes   les petits pois verts

les aubergines noires   les tomates rouges   les oignons blancs

les radis roses   les pommes de terre jaunes   les cerises rouges

2 Compte les fruits et les légumes et réponds aux questions.

a   Il y a combien de poire**s** verte**s**?   *Il y a cinq poires vertes.* _____

b   Il y a combien de tomate**s** rouge**s**? _____

c   Il y a combien de pomme**s** de terre jaune**s**? _____

d   Il y a combien de petit**s** poi**s** vert**s**? _____

e   Il y a combien de banane**s** jaune**s**? _____

f   Il y a combien d'aubergine**s** noire**s**? _____

g   Il y a combien de fraise**s** rouge**s**? _____

h   Il y a combien de pomme**s** rouge**s**? _____

un   deux   trois   quatre   cinq   six   sept   huit   neuf   dix   onze   douze

vocabulaire

Il y a combien de ...? = How many ... are there?   **Il y a ...** = There is/there are ... .

After **combien** you need to use **de** or **d'**. Can you work out when we use **d'**?

notes

En général, pour mettre un nom ou un adjectif au pluriel on ajoute un '**s' muet** au nom et à l'adjectif.

Getting the basics right © CILT 2001. May be photocopied only within the purchasing institution.

1   Colorie les animaux:

les beaux chats noirs   les beaux éléphants gris   les belles tortues vertes
les beaux canards verts   les belles souris blanches   les beaux lapins blancs
les beaux chiens gris   les beaux serpents noirs   les beaux oiseaux bleus
les beaux poissons rouges   les belles grenouilles vertes les belles coccinelles rouges

2   Compte les animaux et réponds aux questions.

a   Il y a combien de chat**s** noir**s**?   *Il y a quatre chats noirs.* _____

b   Il y a combien de canard**s** vert**s**?   _____

c   Il y a combien de chien**s** gris?   _____

d   Il y a combien de poisson**s** rouge**s**? _____

e   Il y a combien d'éléphant**s** gris?   _____

f   Il y a combien de souri**s** blanche**s**? _____

g   Il y a combien de serpent**s** noir**s**?   _____

h   Il y a combien de grenouille**s** vert**s**?_____

un   deux   trois   quatre   cinq   six   sept   huit   neuf   dix   onze   douze

notes   En général, pour mettre un nom au pluriel on ajoute un 's' au nom.

Exception: on ajoute '**x**' à oiseau: les oiseau**x**. En général, pour mettre un adjectif au pluriel on ajoute un '**s**' à l'adjectif. Exception: On ajoute **x** à beau: beau**x**.

1 Suis le code de a à h et complète l'exercice. Attention! Mets les noms des animaux au pluriel.

j'adore	j'aime	je n'aime pas	je déteste

a les serpents	**b** les lapins	**c** les grenouilles	**d** les canards
e les chats	**f** les tortues	**g** les souris	**h** les araignées

a	*Je déteste les serpents.*
b	
c	
d	
e	
f	
g	
h	

2 C'est à toi maintenant. Indique dans le coin de chaque case si tu aimes ces animaux.

Singulier	Pluriel	Singulier	Pluriel
le/la/l'	les	un/une	des

1 Mets au pluriel:

une aubergine	*des aubergines*	une carotte	
un concombre	*des*	un petit pois	
une courgette		un chou-fleur	
un poivron		un oignon	
un livre		une fenêtre	
un sac		un stylo	
une télévision		une chaise	
un cahier		un ordinateur	

2 Mets au pluriel:

le kiwi	*les kiwis*	la pêche	
la poire		l'abricot	
la pomme		la cerise	
le melon		le citron	
la fraise		la mangue	
le père	*les pères*	la mère	
la femme		le frère	
la fille		la tante	
l'oncle		le garçon	

3 Mets au pluriel. Attention: des ou les?

un pull	*des pulls*	le costume	
la robe		une chemise	
le T-shirt		un jean	
une chaussure		la chaussette	
un chat	*des chats*	une tortue	
le chien	*les chiens*	le lion	
un hamster		un serpent	
la grenouille		l'araignée	

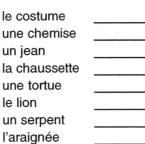

1　　Complète et colorie ces dessins.

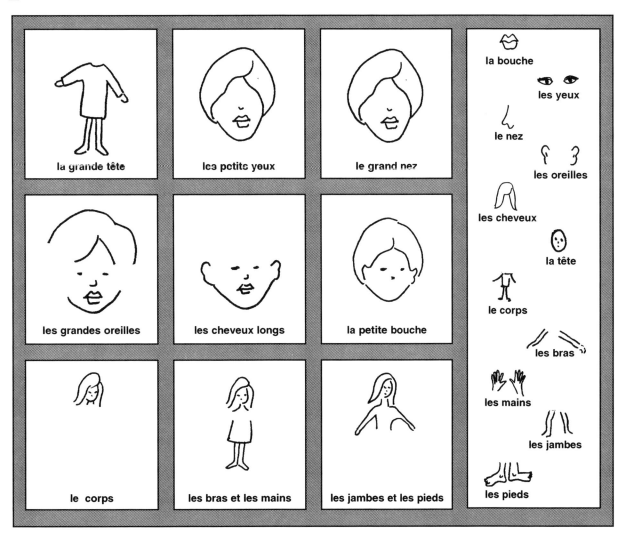

la grande tête | les petits yeux | le grand nez
les grandes oreilles | les cheveux longs | la petite bouche
le corps | les bras et les mains | les jambes et les pieds

la bouche
les yeux
le nez
les oreilles
les cheveux
la tête
le corps
les bras
les mains
les jambes
les pieds

2　　Dessine et colorie le monstre.

Mon monstre

Il a trois têtes roses,
neuf yeux verts,
trois nez rouges,
trois bouches rouges,
six oreilles grises,
le corps bleu,
quatre longs bras verts,
quatre petites mains jaunes,
deux longues jambes vertes
deux pieds noirs.

3　　Décris un monstre à ton partenaire.
Il/elle doit suivre tes instructions et
doit dessiner et colorier ton monstre.

Getting the basics right © CILT 2001. May be photocopied only within the purchasing institution.

1 Dessine une figure avec les chiffres de un à huit. Regarde et copie.

Dessine le front avec le numéro 1.
le nez avec le numéro 4.
la bouche avec le numéro 5.
le menton avec le numéro 6
le cou avec le numéro 7.
les cheveux avec treize numéros 8.
l'œil avec le numéro 2.
l'oreille avec le numéro 3.

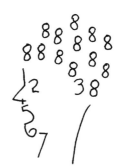

2 ## Le jeu de Picasso

Est-ce que tu sais dessiner une figure avec les yeux bandés? Demande à tes amis de te guider.

Exemple: Dessine l'œil. Commence en haut …

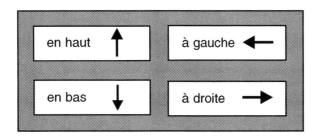

3 Complète ce dessin et nomme les différentes parties de la figure.

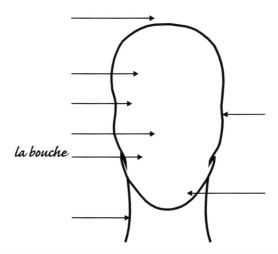

la bouche

vocabulaire	**dessiner** = to draw **écris** = write
	commence = start

notes	*Le pluriel de 'œil' est 'yeux'. Le pluriel de 'cheveu' est ' cheveux'.*
	Notice that in French 'hair' is referred to in the plural: **les cheveux.**

1   Complète et colorie les dessins.

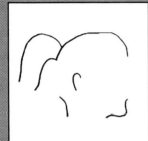

La fille a les yeux bleus,
un petit nez,
une bouche rouge,
les cheveux blonds.

Le garçon a les yeux verts
un grand nez,
une bouche rose,
et les cheveux noirs.

Le clown a de petits yeux noirs.
un grand nez rond et rouge,
une immense bouche rouge,
de grandes oreilles,
et les cheveux roux.

Monsieur Junot a les yeux noirs,
de petites oreilles,
une moustache noire,
une bouche rose,
et les cheveux noirs.
Il porte un chapeau rouge.

Mademoiselle Mireille a les yeux
verts, un petit nez, une petite
bouche rouge, de petites oreilles,
et de longs cheveux blonds.
Elle porte des lunettes roses.

la fille

le garçon

les yeux

le nez

la bouche

les oreilles

les cheveux

la moustache

les lunettes

le chapeau

Getting the basics right © CILT 2001. May be photocopied only within the purchasing institution.

1 Complète et colorie les dessins.

Monsieur Didier a les yeux verts
et une moustache grise.
Il porte une veste verte,
une chemise jaune,
un pantalon noir,
une cravate jaune et verte,
un grand chapeau rouge
et des chaussures noires.
Il tient un parapluie bleu dans la
main droite.

Madame Fanfan a les yeux
bleus,
un petit nez,
une grande bouche,
et de longs cheveux blonds.
Elle porte des lunettes roses,
une robe à pois rouges,
et des chaussures brunes.
Elle tient un bouquet de fleurs
rouges.

Mademoiselle Rosalie porte un
chapeau rose,
une jupe à rayures bleues et
jaunes,
un T-shirt bleu,
et des baskets blanches.
Elle a les cheveux bruns.
les yeux verts,
une petite bouche.
Elle tient un petit sac noir.

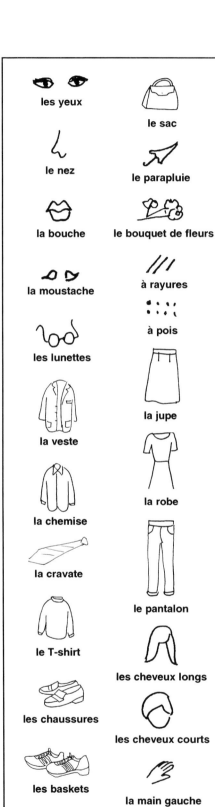

les yeux

le nez

la bouche

la moustache

les lunettes

la veste

la chemise

la cravate

le T-shirt

les chaussures

les baskets

le chapeau

le sac

le parapluie

le bouquet de fleurs

à rayures

à pois

la jupe

la robe

le pantalon

les cheveux longs

les cheveux courts

la main gauche

la main droite

1 La figure et le corps

Chaque équipe a besoin de ces trois toupies.
Découpe les toupies et colorie-les.

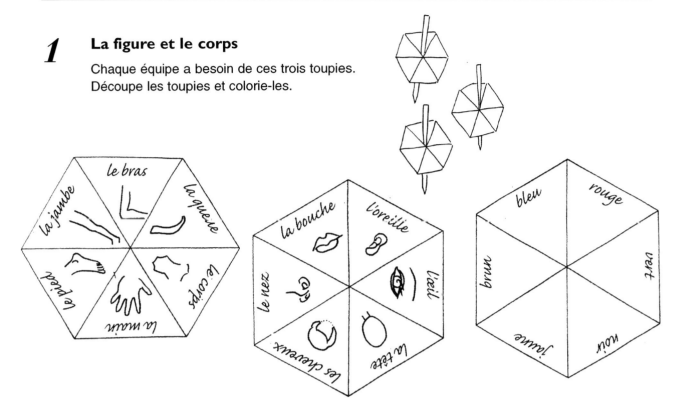

2

Chacun à son tour fait tourner les trois toupies. Les membres de chaque équipe dessinent les parties du corps ou de la tête indiquées par les toupies. Ils écrivent au bas de la page la description.

3

Exemple: *Mon Extra Terrestre a deux têtes rouges et une tête bleue. Une queue noire. Deux pieds bleus. Deux pieds jaunes. Quatre yeux verts. Une bouche jaune, etc.*

L'Extra Terrestre le plus drôle avec sa description écrite correctement gagne.

La classe vote:

Premier prix

Deuxième prix

Troisième prix

Quelques expressions utiles:

vocabulaire		
C'est mon tour. = It's my turn.	**dessine** = draw
C'est ton tour. = It's your turn.	**colorie** = colour in
Tourne la toupie. = Spin the top.	**Je gagne!** = I'm winning!
Passe-moi les feutres. = Pass me the felt tips.	**Tu gagnes!** = You're winning!
joue = play	

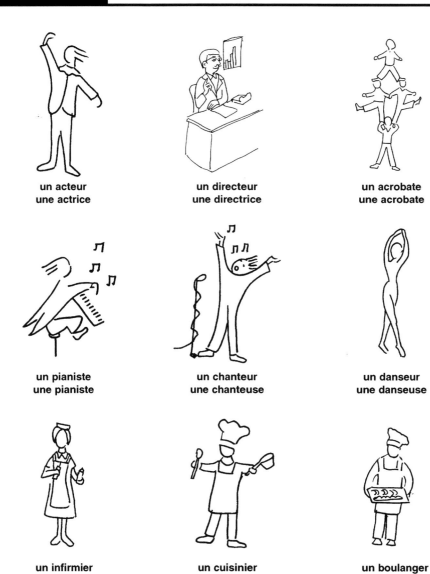

un acteur
une actrice

un directeur
une directrice

un acrobate
une acrobate

un pianiste
une pianiste

un chanteur
une chanteuse

un danseur
une danseuse

un infirmier
une infirmière

un cuisinier
une cuisinière

un boulanger
une boulangère

1 Le professeur divise la classe en deux équipes. Chaque joueur à son tour mime un métier. Le professeur demande: 'Qu'est-ce qu'il/elle est?'. La classe devine et dit: 'Il/Elle est …' et nomme le métier. L'équipe qui devine correctement, gagne un point.

vocabulaire				
Qu'est-ce qu'il est?	= What is he?	**il**	= he	
Il est ………	= He is ………	**elle**	= she	
Qu'est-ce qu'elle est?	= What is she?	**ils**	= they (masculine)	
Elle est ………	= She is ………	**elles**	= they (feminine)	
Qu'est-ce qu'ils sont?	= What are they?			
Ils sont ………	= They are ………			
Qu'est-ce qu'elles sont?	= What are they?			
Elles sont ………	= They are ………			

notes	Even if you are describing one billion girls and just one boy you need to use **ils**!

Joue à ce jeu de mime avec ton professeur et tes camarades .

Pour deviner ce qu'un garcon ou une fille mime, dis: 'Tu es + (adjectif masculin ou féminin)'.
Pour deviner ce que ton professeur mime, dis: 'Vous êtes+ (adjectif masculin ou féminin)'.
Pour deviner ce que des enfants miment, dis: 'Vous êtes + (adjectif masculin ou féminin + **s** muet).

1   Les adjectifs masculins: Devine ce que je suis. Devine ce que nous sommes.

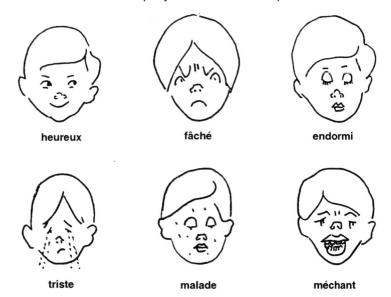

2   Les adjectifs féminins: Devine ce que je suis. Devine ce que nous sommes.

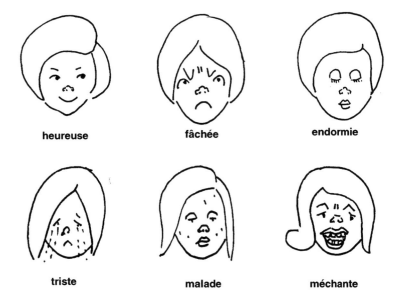

| Tu es .... ? | Vous êtes .... ? | Vous êtes .... + s? |

vocabulaire	**fâché/e** = angry	**triste** = sad
	endormi/e = asleep	**malade** = ill
	heureux/heureuse = happy	**méchant/e** = bad/naughty

Narrateur, Monsieur Bertrand, David, Michelle,
Lina, Roger, Sophie, Henri et Jeanette

[Monsieur Bertrand entre dans la classe]

■ *M. Bertrand:*   Bonjour les enfants.

LES ENFANTS: BONJOUR MONSIEUR BERTRAND.

[David et Michelle rient]

■ *M. Bertrand:*   Silence! ... *Now let me see if you can remember yesterday's lesson. I shall point to different things in the classroom.* Je montre du doigt des objets différents dans la classe. David, qu'est-ce que c'est? [*points at table*]

○ *David:*   C'est une table.

■ *M. Bertrand:*   Très bien, et ça Michelle, qu'est-ce que c'est?

➤ *Michelle:*   Une gomme.

■ *M. Bertrand:*   Il faut dire: 'C'est une gomme. Regarde Michelle, qu'est-ce que c'est? [*points at ruler*]

➤ *Michelle:*   C'est un règle.

■ *M. Bertrand:*   Non! Non! Non!

➤ *Michelle:*   C'est une règle.

■ *M. Bertrand:*   Oui, une règle. Très bien. Regarde, **une** règle, **une** table, **une** chaise, **un** crayon, **un** stylo, **une** fenêtre, **un** sac. *Do you understand?*

Vous comprenez?

[Les enfants rient]

■ *M. Bertrand:*   Silence! Ça suffit! *Now I'll continue.* Je continue. Qu'est-ce que c'est, Lina? [*points at book*]

▲ *Lina:*   C'est un livre.

■ *M. Bertrand:*   Oui, très bien. *Now can you say the noun and the colour.* Le nom et la couleur. *Say: 'He looks at the red books.'*

▲ *Lina:*   Il regarde les rouges livres.

56

Part 2 C   8   Poisson d'avril! (*suite*)

■ *M. Bertrand:*   Non! Non! Non! *In French you say the noun first then the colour.* Le nom d'abord, puis la couleur. Il regarde **les** livres rouges.

[Les enfants rient]

■ *M. Bertrand:*   Silence! Ça suffit! *Roger, say: 'I love the little black cats. Use* petit – small. *Remember:* grand *and* petit *are placed before the noun; the colour after the noun. Remember* grand, grande, petit, petite *and 'the' is* le *or* la.

[Les enfants rient]

∧ *Roger:*   J'aime les petits chats noirs.

■ *M. Bertrand:*   Très bien, mais silence! Ça suffit! Pourquoi riez-vous? Combien de gommes y a t-il Julien? [*points at 3 rubbers*]

⇨ *Julien:*   Il y a trois gommes.

■ *M. Bertrand:*   Très bien.

[Les enfants rient]

■ *M. Bertrand:*   Silence! *Now I want you to form a sentence. Say: 'I play with the blue pen.'*

Sophie: Je joue avec le stylo bleu.

■ *M. Bertrand:*   Bravo, c'est super!

[Les enfants rient]

■ *M. Bertrand:*   Qu'est-ce que je porte, Henri?

Narrateur: M. Bertrand montre du doigt sa cravate rouge.

♥ *Henri:*   Vous portez une cravate rouge.

■ *M. Bertrand:*   Je porte une superbe cravate rouge. *Now say: 'On top of a beautiful white shirt.'*

♥ *Henri:*   Vous portez une superbe cravate rouge sur une très belle chemise blanche.

[Les enfants rient et applaudissent]

■ *M. Bertrand*   C'est excellent Henri. Bravo! Mais ça suffit, les enfants! Pourquoi riez-vous? Vous n'aimez pas ma belle chemise?

Henri, assieds-toi. Jeanette, cesse de rire!

[M. Bertrand montre du doigt ses chaussures]

■ *M. Bertrand*   *Jeanette, say: 'these shoes'.*

[Les enfants rient]

Getting the basics right © CILT 2001. May be photocopied only within the purchasing institution.

Getting the basics right © CILT 2001. May be photocopied only within the purchasing institution.

■ *M. Bertrand:*   Jeanette, allons j'attends! Cessez de rire!

✔ *Jeanette:*   Cette chaussure.

■ *M. Bertrand:*   Non, non, non! Cette – singulier. Ces – pluriel. Ces chaussures.

[Les enfants rient.]

■ *M. Bertrand:*   Voyons! Cessez de rire, les enfants! Lina, quelle heure est-il?

▲ *Lina:*   Il est neuf heures dix.

■ *M. Bertrand:*   Oui, c'est très bien. Mais pourquoi riez-vous? Lina, quelle est la date d'aujourd'hui?

▲ *Lina:*   Le premier avril.

Narrateur: M. Bertrand touche son dos. Son visage est tout rouge. Il attrape le poisson d'avril que les enfants ont accroché sur sa chemise. Les enfants cessent de rire. Ils ont peur.

[M. Bertrand éclate de rire!]

■ *M. Bertrand:*   Ha! Ha! Ha! Je comprends pourquoi vous riez. Ha! Ha! Ha! C'est le premier avril!

LES ENFANTS: Poisson d'avril, Monsieur Bertrand!

Pour faire un Poisson d'avril

Dessine et colorie un poisson de 25cm de long. Fais un petit trou sur sa queue. Enfile une ficelle. Attache la ficelle sur une épingle de sûreté.

Voici ma famille

1 Suis l'exemple et dessine ta famille ou ta famille imaginaire.

2 Indique la parenté des différents membres de ta famille en utilisant:
mon, **ma** ou **mes** (**mon** père, **ma** mère, etc).

notes					
mon:	père	frère	grand-père	oncle	cousin
ma:	mère	sœur	grand-mère	tante	cousine

Getting the basics right © CILT 2001. May be photocopied only within the purchasing institution.

1   Encercle en noir les noms qui sont au pluriel et écris **mes**.

2   Encercle en vert les noms qui commencent par une voyelle ou un 'h muet' et écris **mon**.

3   Encercle en bleu les noms qui sont au masculin singulier et qui ne commencent pas par une voyelle ou un 'h muet' et écris **mon**.

4   Encercle en rouge les noms qui sont au féminin singulier et qui ne commencent pas par une voyelle ou un 'h muet' et écris **ma**.

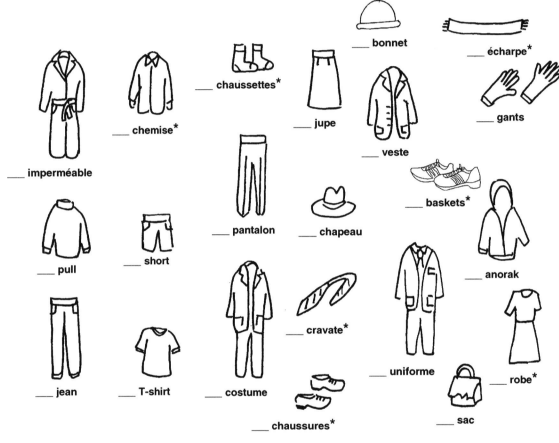

___ bonnet

___ écharpe*

___ chaussettes*

___ jupe

___ gants

___ chemise*

___ veste

___ imperméable

___ baskets*

___ pantalon

___ chapeau

___ pull

___ short

___ anorak

___ cravate*

___ uniforme

___ jean

___ T-shirt

___ costume

___ robe*

___ sac

___ chaussures*

Attention! * = nom féminin

vocabulaire	the	my
	les	mes
	l'	mon
	le	mon
	la	ma

notes

In French, jeans, trousers, pants, tights, pyjamas and shorts are referred to in the singular: **un jean, un pantalon, une culotte, un collant, un pyjama, un short.**

Most articles of clothing ending with 'e' are feminine. (* = fem). Exception: **un imperméable, un costume, un uniforme.**
All articles of clothing in the singular not ending with an 'e' are masculine.

1 Dessine ton portrait. Indique avec des flèches les différentes parties de ta tête et de ton corps. Ecris-les en utilisant les adjectifs possessifs: **mon, ma** et **mes**.

Moi!

Masculin *mon*: pied nez corps dos bras cou ventre œil

Féminin *ma*: tête main jambe bouche oreille

Pluriel *mes*: cheveux

notes

Oreille is a feminine noun, but it starts with a vowel, so we say '**mon oreille**'.
Cheveux: hair in French, is referred to in the plural so we say: '**mes cheveux**' (unless you are talking about one hair only).
The plural of **œil** is **yeux**. So: **Mon œil** becomes in the plural **mes yeux**.

1   Dessine les membres de ta famille ou de ta famille imaginaire dans ces cadres. Présente-les en utilisant les adjectifs possessifs **mon** ou **ma.** Ecris leur nom, leur âge et décris-les.

C'est mon _____: père   frère   oncle   grand-père   cousin
Il s'appelle _____   **Il a** _____ **ans**
Il est _____   *beau* = beautiful   *intelligent* = intelligent   *mignon* = cute
                   moche = ghastly   *adorable* = adorable   *méchant* = naughty

C'est ma _____: mère   sœur   tante   grand-mère   cousine
Elle s'appelle _____   **Elle a** _____ **ans**
Elle est _____   belle   intelligente   mignonne
                        moche   adorable   méchante

C'est *ma mère*   .
Elle s'appelle *Claire*   .
Elle a *35*   ans.
Elle est *belle*   .

C'est_____.
_____ s'appelle_____.
_____ a_____ ans.
_____ est_____.

C'est_____.
_____ s'appelle_____.
_____ a_____ ans.
_____ est_____.

C'est _____.
_____ s'appelle_____.
_____ a _____ ans.
_____ est_____.

C'est _____.
_____ s'appelle_____.
_____ a _____ ans.
_____ est_____.

---

vocabulaire   **il** = he   **elle** = she
                    il s'appelle = he is called
                    il a X ans = he is X years old

1   Indique dans les cases si tu aimes ou si tu n'aimes pas ces aliments et ces boissons.

| j'aime ♡ | je n'aime pas ♡̶ |

☐ mon / ton   melon

☐ ma / ta   soupe

☐ ma / ta   salade

☐ mon / ton   avocat

☐ mon / ton   poisson

☐ ma / ta   viande

☐ ma / ta   dinde

☐ mon / ton   poulet

☐ mes / tes   frites

☐ mes / tes   carottes

☐ mes / tes   petits pois

☐ mon / ton   chou-fleur

☐ mon / ton   gâteau

☐ ma / ta   glace

☐ ma / ta   tarte

☐ mes / tes   fruits

☐ mon / ton   vin

☐ mon / ton   coca

☐ mon / ton   jus

☐ mon / ton   eau

2   **Conversation au restaurant**

Demande à ton/ta partenaire si il ou elle aime ces aliments et ces boissons.

– Tu aimes ton/ta/tes … ?

Oui, J'aime mon/ma/mes …	**Non,** Je n'aime pas mon/ma/mes …
C'est bon! It's good!	**Ce n'est pas bon!** It's not good!
C'est délicieux! It's delicious!	**C'est dégoûtant!** It's disgusting!

1 Joue au 'Morpion' avec tes amis. Pour mettre une croix ou un rond dans la case de ton choix il faut suivre l'exemple et faire quatre phrases:

'C'est mon/ma … . Il/elle s'appelle … .
Il/elle est [+ *couleur*]. Il/elle est [+ *adjectif*].

2 Ecris quatre phrases sur chaque animal.

a _C'est mon chat. Il s'appelle Poussy. Il est blanc et noir. Il est mignon._

b _____

c _____

d _____

e _____

f _____

g _____

h _____

i _____

vocabulaire	C'est mon (ma) … . Il (Elle) s'appelle … . Il (Elle) est [+ couleur].
méchant(e) = naughty	**beau (belle)** = beautiful **mignon(ne)** = mignon
grand(e) = big	**petit(e)** = small **adorable** = adorable
intelligent(e) = intelligent	**gros(se)** = fat **câlin(e)** = cuddly

1   Colorie cette maison, puis plie la page sur la ligne pointillée.

2   Pour ouvrir les portes et les fenêtres, coupe sur les lignes pointillées et fais un pli sur les grosses lignes. Ouvre les fenêtres et les portes et écris le nom des pièces avec 'mon' ou 'ma'.

3   Maintenant, écris quelques lignes pour décrir ta maison ou ta maison imaginaire. Commence en écrivant:
'Dans ma maison il y a ...'
N'oublie pas d'ajouter un 's' aux noms et aux adjectifs qui sont au pluriel.

vocabulaire

Féminin:	**chambre:** bedroom	**salle de bains:** bathroom	**salle à manger:** dining room
	cuisine: kitchen	**cave:** cellar	
Masculin:	**salon:** living room	**grenier:** attic **jardin:** garden	**garage:** garage

- -

Dans ma maison il y a _____

_____

_____

_____

_____

1 Ecris au pluriel. **Attention!** Ecris le nom puis la couleur.

a ma petite trousse verte   *mes petites trousses vertes* _____

b mon petit cahier jaune _____

c ma grande table blanche _____

d mon grand sac noir _____

e ma bonne pomme rouge   *mes bonnes pommes rouges* _____

f ma bonne pastèque _____

g ma bonne carotte _____

h mon bon melon jaune _____

i mon bon citron vert _____

j mon beau T-shirt vert   *mes beaux T-shirts verts* _____

k ma belle robe grise   *mes belles robes grises* _____

l mon beau pantalon _____

m ma belle chemise jaune _____

n ma belle jupe rouge _____

o mon beau pull noir _____

p ma belle tortue grise _____

q mon beau lapin blanc _____

r ma belle souris blanche _____

s mon beau canard vert _____

t mon beau chat blanc _____

Masculin		Féminin	
Singulier	**Pluriel**	**Singulier**	**Pluriel**
beau	beaux	belle	belles
bon	bons	bonne	bonnes
grand	grands	grande	grandes
petit	petits	petite	petites

notes	In general to make the plural of a noun or an adjective, you must add a 'silent **s**' to the noun and the adjective. Exception: you have to add a 'silent **x**' to **beau: beaux**.

> plus … que = more … than
> moins … que = less … than
> aussi … que = as … as

petit/petite	small
gros/grosse	fat
haut/haute	tall
léger/légère	light
lourd/lourde	heavy
beau/belle	beautiful
intelligent/intelligente	intelligent
stupide/stupide	stupid
lent/lente	slow
rapide/rapide	fast
méchant/méchante	naughty

la fourmi

l'araignée

l'écureuil

la tortue

la souris

le serpent

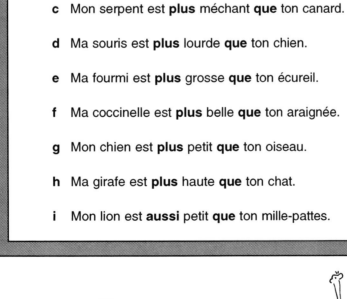

1 **Coche la case si c'est vrai.** ☑

a Mon lapin est **plus** rapide **que** ta tortue. ☐

b Mon singe est **plus** intelligent **que** ton poisson. ☐

c Mon serpent est **plus** méchant **que** ton canard. ☐

d Ma souris est **plus** lourde **que** ton chien. ☐

e Ma fourmi est **plus** grosse **que** ton écureil. ☐

f Ma coccinelle est **plus** belle **que** ton araignée. ☐

g Mon chien est **plus** petit **que** ton oiseau. ☐

h Ma girafe est **plus** haute **que** ton chat. ☐

i Mon lion est **aussi** petit **que** ton mille-pattes. ☐

le singe

le mille-pattes

le chat

l'oiseau

le lapin

le canard

le chien

le lion

la girafe

le poisson

la coccinelle

---

plus ... que ... = more than
plus **beau/belle que** = more beautiful than
plus **méchant/méchante que** = more naughty than
plus **intelligent/intelligente que** = more intelligent than
plus **grand/grande que** = bigger (more big) than

---

moins ... que ... = less than
moins **beau/belle que** = less beautiful than
moins **méchant/méchante que** = less naughty than
moins **intelligent/intelligente que** = less intelligent than
moins **grand/grande que** = less big

---

aussi ... que ... = as ... as
aussi **beau/belle que** = as beautiful as
aussi **méchant/méchante que** = as naughty
aussi **intelligent/intelligente que** = as intelligent as
aussi **grand/grande que** = as big as

---

1   Ecris en anglais.

a   Mon chat est **plus** grand **que** ton chat   _My cat is bigger than your cat._

b   Ma robe est **moins** belle **que** ta robe.   _____

c   Mon frère est **aussi** petit **que** ton frère.   _____

d   Ma soeur est **plus** méchante **que** ta sœur.   _____

e   Mon père est **plus** intelligent **que** ton père.   _____

f   Mon chien est **plus** mignon **que** ton chien.   _____

g   Marie est **aussi** bonne **que** Julie.   _____

h   Jean est **plus** idiot **que** Paul.   _____

i   Daniel est **moins** grand **que** Fred.   _____

j   Suzie est **aussi** intelligente **qu'**Amira.   _____

k   Rosie est **plus** mignonne **que** Tom!   _____

l   Véronique est **moins** petite **que** Louis.   _____

---

vocabulaire

grand/grande = big	**beau/belle** = beautiful
petit/petite = small	**méchant/méchante** = naughty
intelligent/intelligente = clever	**mignon/mignonne** = cute
bon/bonne = good	**idiot/idiote** = idiotic

1 Encercle avec une ligne noire les noms au pluriel et écris **ces**.

2 Encercle avec une ligne rouge les noms au féminin singulier et écris **cette**.

3 Encercle avec une ligne verte les noms masculins qui commencent par une voyelle ou un 'h muet' et écris **cet**.

4 Encercle avec une ligne bleue les noms au masculin singulier qui ne commencent pas par une voyelle ou un 'h muet' et écris **ce**.

les	ces
l' (masc)	cet
le	ce
la	cette

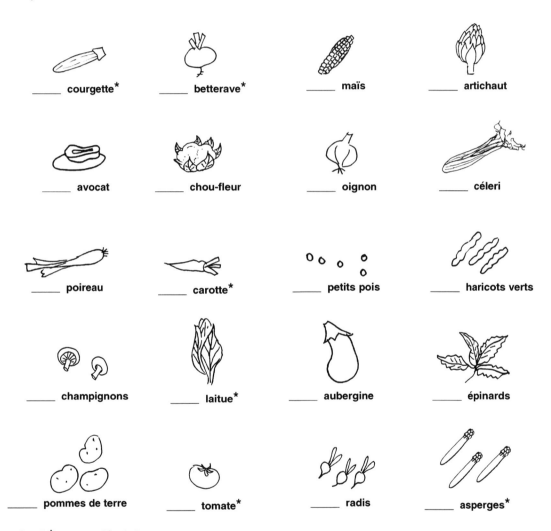

_____ courgette*   _____ betterave*   _____ maïs   _____ artichaut

_____ avocat   _____ chou-fleur   _____ oignon   _____ céleri

_____ poireau   _____ carotte*   _____ petits pois   _____ haricots verts

_____ champignons   _____ laitue*   _____ aubergine   _____ épinards

_____ pommes de terre   _____ tomate*   _____ radis   _____ asperges*

Attention! * = nom féminin

---

vocabulaire

les légumes = the vegetables
ce/cet/cette = this or that
ces = these or those

---

notes

All names of vegetables ending with an 'e' in the singular are feminine nouns.
Exception: **un concombre**.
All names of vegetables not ending with an 'e' in the singular are masculine nouns.

Blockbuster

1 Joue à 'Blockbuster' avec tes camarades. Utilise l'adjectif démonstratif 'ce, cet, cette ou ces' avant de nommer l'animal qui est dans l'hexagone de ton choix.

Exemple: *ce serpent*

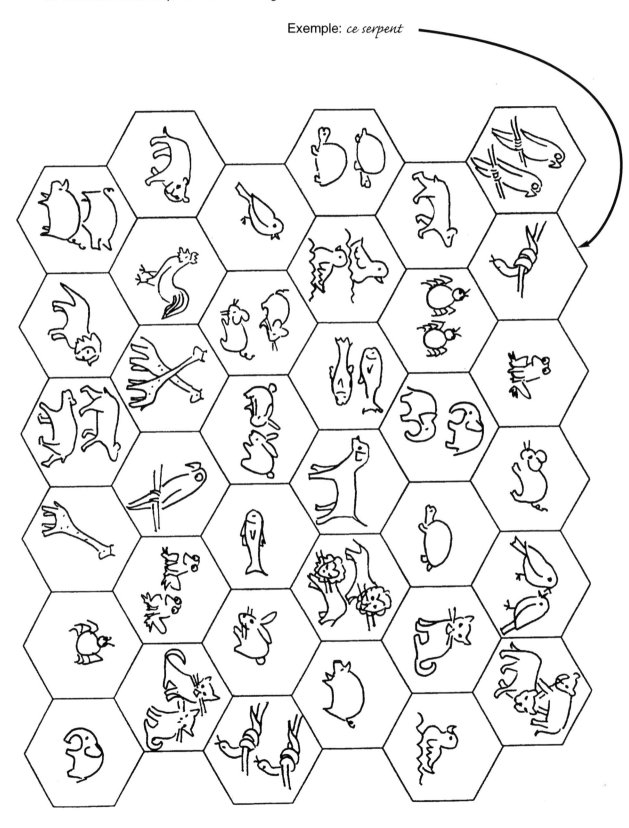

Il est une heure. Notice that **heure** is a feminine noun.
Il est deux heures. Notice that when it is more than 'one hour' we have to add an 's' to **heure.**
Carry on like this until you reach: **Il est onze heures.**

il est une heure   **il est dix heures**   **il est quatre heures**   **il est cinq heures**

There are special words for midday (**midi**) and midnight (**minuit**):

il est midi   **il est minuit**

1 A toi maintenant. Quelle heure est-il? Ecris la réponse.

a   b   c   d

_____ _____ _____ _____

 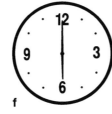  

e   f   g   h

_____ _____ _____ _____

i   j   k   l

_____ _____ _____ _____

vocabulaire	**Quelle heure est-il?** = What's the time?
	Il est ... heure/s. = It is ... o'clock.

1

a To say minutes past the hour: use number of hours + **heure/s** + number of minutes.

il est six heures dix

il est sept heures cinq

il onze heures vingt-cinq

b To say minutes to the hour (after the half hour): use number of hours it will be + **heure/s** + **moins** + number of minutes.

Example: for 'quarter to': number of hours it will be + **heure/s** + **moins le quart**:

il est une heure moins le quart

il est dix heures moins cinq

il est deux heures moins vingt

c To say quarter past: use number of hours + **heure/s** + **et quart**:

il est une heure et quart

il est trois heures et quart

il est quatre heures et quart

d To say half-past: use number of hours + **heure/s** + **et demie**:

il est neuf heures et demie

il est huit heures et demie

il est onze heures et demie

2 A toi maintenant. Quelle heure est-il?

a

b

c

d

e

_____ _____ _____ _____ _____

_____ _____ _____ _____ _____

1	premier	8	huit	15	quinze	22	vingt-deux
2	deux	9	neuf	16	seize	23	vingt-trois
3	trois	**10**	**dix**	17	dix-sept	24	vingt-quatre
4	quatre	11	onze	18	dix-huit	**30**	**trente**
5	cinq	12	douze	19	dix-neuf	31	trente et un
6	six	13	treize	**20**	**vingt**		
7	sept	14	quatorze	21	vingt et un		

1 Quelle est la date aujourd'hui?

01/10 *C'est le premier octobre.*   17/5 _____

11/7 *C'est le*   .   13/10 _____

15/8 _____   27/7 _____

04/6 _____   30/2 _____

17/3 _____   13/12 _____

26/9 _____   18/4 _____

01/1 _____   09/6 _____

2 Demande à dix camarades: Quelle est la date de ton anniversaire? Fais une liste des anniversaires.

vocabulaire	**janvier** = January	**mai** = May	**septembre** = September
	février = February	**juin** = June	**octobre** = October
	mars = March	**juillet** = July	**novembre** = November
	avril = April	**août** = August	**décembre** = December

notes	Don't use capital letters to write the months.

Quelle heure est-il?

01:00	Il est **une** heure.
09:45	Il est dix heure**s** moins le quart.
02:30	Il est deux heure**s** et demie.
07:15	Il est sept heure**s** et quart.

1 Quelle heure est-il?

10:15	*Il est dix heures et quart.*
01:30	
08:15	
03:30	
12:00	
04:30	
06:30	
01:45	
05:15	

01:00	
02:05	*Il est deux heures cinq.*
09:40	
01:35	
06:10	
10:25	*Il est dix heures vingt-cinq.*
04:12	
11:20	
02:50	

notes	There are special words for midday (**midi**) and midnight (**minuit**).

1 Colorie ces vêtements.

2 Relie les vêtements de 1 à 12 avec une ligne bleue et de 13 à 20 avec une ligne rouge.

1 ce beau manteau bleu	13 cette belle ceinture grise
2 ce beau chapeau rouge	14 cette belle veste bleue
3 ces beaux gants verts	15 cette belle cravate jaune
4 ces belles baskets blanches	16 cette belle chemise verte
5 ce beau T-shirt orange	17 ces belles chaussures noires
6 ce beau sweatshirt vert	18 ces belles chaussettes roses
7 ce beau short noir	19 cette belle jupe rouge
8 ce beau jogging bleu	20 cette belle robe orange
9 ce beau pantalon gris	
10 ce beau jean bleu	
11 ce beau pull jaune	
12 ce beau bonnet rouge	

Première partie

Narrateur: Le roi et la reine sont malheureux parce qu'ils n'ont pas d'enfants.

✔ *La reine:*   Oh! Je voudrais tant avoir un enfant.

▲ *Le roi:*   Oui, moi aussi, je voudrais tant avoir un enfant.

Narrateur: Après de longues années d'attente, la reine est enceinte. Une petite fille est née. Le roi est très heureux. Il offre une grande fête pour la naissance de sa fille.

Il invite toutes les fées du royaume pour qu'elles dotent l'enfant des qualités les plus merveilleuses. Malheureusement il oublie d'inviter la fée Carabosse.

★ *Le soldat:*   Le roi et la reine vous invitent au palais, le dimanche cinq juillet, pour célébrer la naissance de leur fille.

Narrateur: Toutes les fées sont contentes. Elles se préparent pour la grande fête. La fée Carabosse est très fâchée. Elle est furieuse! Elle n'est pas invitée à la fête.

■ *La fée Carabosse:*   Je suis furieuse. Le Roi ne m'a pas invitée à la fête. Ahhhh!

Narrateur: La fête commence. Toutes les fées se mettent en rang pour faire un vœu et toucher la princesse avec leur bâton magique.

La première fée: Elle sera la plus belle.

La deuxième fée: Elle sera la plus douce.

La troisième fée: Elle sera la plus intelligente.

La quatrième fée: Elle sera la plus bonne.

La cinquième fée: Elle sera la plus courageuse.

La sixième fée: Elle sera la plus sympathique.

La septième fée :   Elle sera la plus généreuse.

La huitième fée: Elle sera la plus élégante.

La neuvième fée: Elle sera la plus gentille.

La dixième fée: Elle sera la plus obéissante.

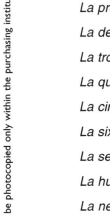

Narrateur: Soudain, une grande ombre noire tombe sur toutes les fées. La fée Carabosse vole sur son balai jusqu'au berceau. Carabosse touche la princesse avec son bâton magique.

■ *Carabosse:*   Un jour, tu te piqueras la main avec un fuseau et tu en mourras!

Narrateur: Elle disparaît. Les fées, le roi et la reine sont consternés. Une gentille fée qui n'a pas fait son vœu s'approche du berceau. Elle touche la princesse avec son bâton magique.

^ *La douzième fée:*   Je ne sais pas annuler le maléfice mais je peux en atténuer les effets. Elle ne mourra pas; elle sera plongée dans un long sommeil de cent ans. Le Prince Charmant viendra la réveiller.

Narrateur: Le roi, pour éviter le malheur, ordonne que les fuseaux soient brûlés dans tout le royaume.

Deuxième partie: Quelques années plus tard

Narrateur: La princesse est devenue la plus belle, la plus douce, la plus intelligente, la plus bonne, la plus courageuse, la plus sympathique, la plus généreuse, la plus obéissante, la plus élégante, la plus gentille, la plus merveilleuse jeune fille du royaume. La voilà dans un vieux donjon. Elle regarde une très vieille femme qui file de la laine.

♥ *La princesse:* Que c'est joli! Je peux essayer?

➤ *La vieille femme:* Oui, mon enfant!

Narrateur: A peine a-t-elle touché le fuseau, qu'elle se pique le doigt et s'endort. Le roi s'endort. La reine s'endort. Les serviteurs s'endorment. Les cuisiniers s'endorment. Les valets s'endorment. Les jardiniers s'endorment. Les chevaux s'endorment. Les chiens s'endorment. Les chats s'endorment. Même les mouches s'endorment sur les murs. Le feu s'immobilise. Autour du château les arbres grandissent. Une barrière immense encercle le château et protège le sommeil de la princesse. La légende se propage. Personne ne peut franchir la barrière.

Troisième partie: Cent ans plus tard

Narrateur: Un beau prince passe près du château. Il connaît la légende. Il est curieux. Il avance sur son cheval près de la barrière. Les branches des arbres s'écartent sur son passage. Il entre dans le jardin. Il arrive au château. Il voit les chiens, les chats et les chevaux, qui dorment. Un silence inquiétant reigne. La porte du château s'ouvre. Il monte au donjon et découvre une merveilleuse princesse. Il se penche sur elle et lui donne un baiser. Elle ouvre les yeux et sourit.

♥ *La princesse:* Mon Prince! Je suis si heureuse de vous voir!

○ *Le Prince:* Ma Princesse! Que vous êtes belle!

Narrateur: Soudain les chiens bondissent. Le roi et la reine se réveillent. Les serviteurs, les cuisiniers, les soldats, les valets, les jardiniers se réveillent. Le château s'anime. Les cuisiniers préparent un superbe festin pour le mariage du Prince Charmant et de la Belle au bois dormant. La joie règne.

1 Chante cette chanson sur l'air de '*London bridge is falling down*'.
Fais les mouvements correspondants.

*S*ur, sous, dans, devant, derrière.
Devant, derrière,
Devant, derrière.
Sur, sous, dans, devant, derrière.
A côté de.

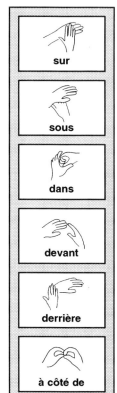

2 Dessine une balle:

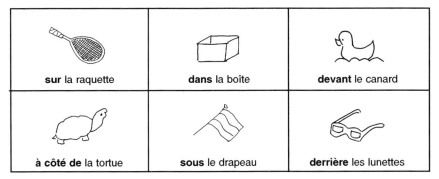

sur la raquette	**dans** la boîte	**devant** le canard
à côté de la tortue	**sous** le drapeau	**derrière** les lunettes

3 Complète les blancs. Sur, sous, dans, devant, derrière ou à côté de …?

Où est le crayon? Le crayon est *derrière* _____ le sac.	Où est le chien? Le chien est _____ la souris.	Où est la règle? La règle est _____ le livre.
Où est la plante? La plante est _____ la télé.	Où est l'oiseau? L'oiseau est _____ la grenouille.	Où est la fille? La fille est _____ la voiture.

4 Suis l'exemple et réponds aux questions.

Où est le chat? *Le chat est* *à côté du chapeau.*	Où est le chat? _____ _____	Où est le chat? _____ _____
Où est le chat? _____ _____	Où est le chat? _____ _____	Où est le chat? _____ _____

Two young men in town

1 Try to remember all the English nouns in this story in the right order.

> Two young men arrived at the port. They went to the nearest **hotel**. There, they asked what sort of amenities there were in the town. They were told there was the **restaurant**, the **bar**, the **café** and the **shop**. Across the **road** there is the **supermarket**. On Thursdays there is the **market**.
>
> They went to the **town centre** and stopped at the **tourist information office**. They asked: 'What is there to do here?' They were told that there is the **park**, the **cinema**, the **theatre**, the **stadium**, the **museum** and the **castle**.
>
> They couldn't decide where to go. The first man wanted to go to the museum, but the second wanted to go to the castle. They started shouting and fighting. The first man got injured and was rushed to the **hospital**. The Police arrested the other man and took him to the **Police Station**.

le port	le Syndicat d'Initiative	l'école	la boucherie
l'hôtel	le jardin public	la maison	la charcuterie
le restaurant	le cinéma	la gare	l'épicerie
le bar	le théâtre	la poste	la pharmacie
le café	le stade	la rue	l'auberge de
le magasin	le musée		jeunesse
le supermarché	le château	l'église	la plage
le marché	l'hôpital	la banque	la piscine
le centre-ville	le commissariat	la boulangerie	

A girl on holiday

2 Try to remember all the English nouns in this story in the right order.

> A girl left **school** and rushed **home** to collect her suitcase. She was going on holiday. She ran to the **railway station**. As soon as she arrived at her destination she stopped at the **post-office** to post a letter. She crossed the **road**. She went past the **church**, then stopped at the **bank**. She went past the **bakery**, the **butcher**, the **delicatessen** and the **greengrocer**. She stopped at the **chemist's** to buy some sun cream. She crossed the road and went into the **youth hostel**. As it was too windy to go to the **beach** she went to the **swimming pool**.

3 Link in your mind all the masculine nouns with the two young men and all the feminine nouns with the girl. Try to learn, in the right order, these two lists of nouns, first in English and then in French.

Make sure you can pronounce all the French words correctly.

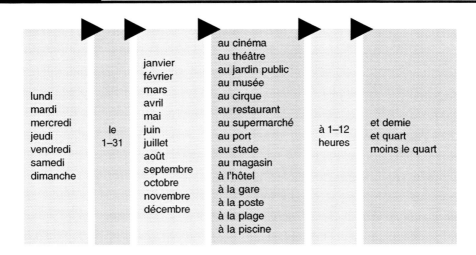

| lundi
mardi
mercredi
jeudi
vendredi
samedi
dimanche | le
1–31 | janvier
février
mars
avril
mai
juin
juillet
août
septembre
octobre
novembre
décembre | au cinéma
au théâtre
au jardin public
au musée
au cirque
au restaurant
au supermarché
au port
au stade
au magasin
à l'hôtel
à la gare
à la poste
à la plage
à la piscine | à 1–12
heures | et demie
et quart
moins le quart |

1 Conversation: Téléphone à un/une camarade de classe. Fixe un rendez-vous.

Pour les téléphones, tu as besoin d'une longue ficelle (6 mètres), deux pots de yaourt en plastique et deux allumettes. Fais un trou au fond de chaque pot. Enfile la ficelle dans les trous. Fais un nœud autour des allumettes à chaque bout. Voilà! C'est facile!

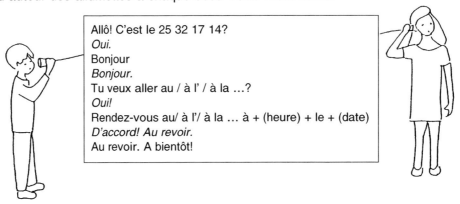

> Allô! C'est le 25 32 17 14?
> *Oui.*
> Bonjour
> *Bonjour.*
> Tu veux aller au / à l' / à la ...?
> *Oui!*
> Rendez-vous au/ à l'/ à la ... à + (heure) + le + (date)
> *D'accord! Au revoir.*
> Au revoir. A bientôt!

2 **L'agent secret!**

Ecris un message secret. Voici le code:

A	B	C	D	E	F	G	H	I	J	K	L	M	N	O	P	Q	R	S	T	U	V	W	X	Y	Z
Z	Y	X	W	V	U	T	S	R	Q	P	O	N	M	L	K	J	I	H	G	F	E	D	C	B	A

Exemple: JE T'AIME = QV G'ZRNV!
Envoie un message secret pour fixer un rendez-vous.

RENDEZ-VOUS A LA POSTE A SIX   HEURES
IVMWVA-ELFH   Z   OZ   KLHGV   Z   HRC   SVFIVH

vocabulaire
le rendez-vous = appointment/date

a RENDEZ-VOUS A LA GARE LUNDI

   IVMWVA-ELFH

b RENDEZ-VOUS AU CINEMA A UNE HEURE

1   **Relie avec une ligne noire** les noms au pluriel au ballon **aux**.

2   **Relie avec une ligne verte** les noms qui commencent par une voyelle ou un 'h muet' au ballon **à l'**.

3   **Relie avec une ligne bleue** les noms au masculin singulier qui ne commencent pas par une voyelle ou un 'h muet' au ballon **au**.

4   **Relie avec une ligne rouge** les noms au féminin singulier qui ne commencent pas par une voyelle ou un 'h muet' au ballon **à la**.

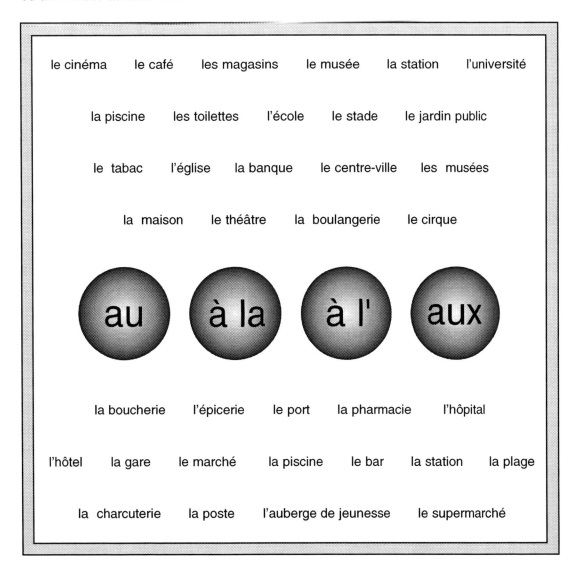

| le cinéma | le café | les magasins | le musée | la station | l'université |

| la piscine | les toilettes | l'école | le stade | le jardin public |

| le tabac | l'église | la banque | le centre-ville | les musées |

| la maison | le théâtre | la boulangerie | le cirque |

au   **à la**   **à l'**   **aux**

| la boucherie | l'épicerie | le port | la pharmacie | l'hôpital |

| l'hôtel | la gare | le marché | la piscine | le bar | la station | la plage |

| la charcuterie | la poste | l'auberge de jeunesse | le supermarché |

| **notes** | à + le = au   à + la = à la   à + l' = à l'   à + les = aux |
| | Many names of shops end in '**-rie**' or '**-ie**' and are feminine, e.g. **la boucherie**. |

banque	poste	château
7/1	12/7	20/10
09:15	11:30	10:00
école	**hôpital**	**port**
24/2	22/8	19/3
08:30	12:45	07:45
jardin public	**musée**	**gare**
12/6	30/5	13/4
12:00	10:15	10:30

1 Joue au 'Morpion' avec tes amis. Pour mettre ta croix ou ton rond dans la case de ton choix tu dois suivre l'exemple: 'Rendez-vous à la gare le treize avril à dix heures et demie.'

2 Maintenant écris huit phrases.

a *Rendez-vous à la banque le sept janvier à neuf heures et quart.*

b _____

c _____

d _____

e _____

f _____

g _____

h _____

i _____

notes			
	au:	**à l':**	**à la:**
	château = castle	**hôpital** = hospital	**banque** = bank
	musée = museum	**école** = school	**poste** = post-office
	jardin public = park		**gare** = railway station
	port = port		

Pour la date écris: le + nombre + mois

il est un**e** heure
et demie = half past

il est quatre heure**s**
et quart = quarter past

moins le quart = quarter to

1   Où ont-ils mal? Qu'est-ce qu'ils disent?

a	b	c	d
l' œil	la tête	les oreilles	le ventre
e	f	g	h
le cœur	la gorge	le pied	le bras

Exemple: J'ai mal au dos.

le dos

a   *J'ai mal à l'œil.* _____

b   _____

c   _____

d   _____

e   _____

f   _____

g   _____

h   _____

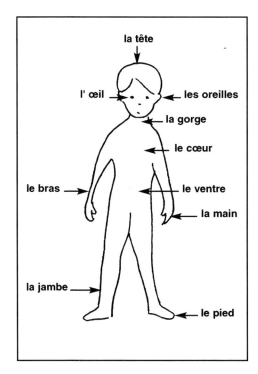

vocabulaire	**Où as-tu mal?** = Where have you got pain?/Where does it hurt? **J'ai mal …** = I have pain …

notes	**à + le = au** **à + la = à la** **à + l' = à l'** **à + les = aux** J'ai mal **à l'** + *noun starting with a, e, i, o, u or h.* J'ai mal **à la** + *feminine noun starting with a consonant.* J'ai mal **au** + *masculine noun starting with a consonant.* J'ai mal **aux** + *plural noun.*

Getting the basics right © CILT 2001. May be photocopied only within the purchasing institution.

1

Colorie les glaces:	a = rouge	c = vert	e = violet	g = orange
	b = jaune	d = blanc	f = marron	h = beige

2   Regarde la liste des spécialités et écris dans les petites cases le prix des glaces et dans les grandes cases le nom des glaces.

Nos spécialités

glace **au** chocolat	18F
glace **au** café	17F
glace **à la** pistache	12F
glace **au** cassis	13F
glace **à la** fraise	19F
glace **à la** vanille	11F
glace **à l'**orange	12F
glace **à l'**ananas	14F

a

19 F

glace à la fraise

b

F

c

F

d
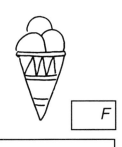
F

e
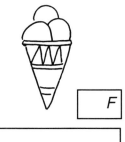
F

f

F

g

F

h
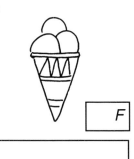
F

3   **Conversation**

Travaille avec ton partenaire pour faire des conversations chez le marchand de glaces. Regarde la liste des parfums et des prix.

Je voudrais une glace, s'il vous plaît.   *Quel parfum?*
Une glace _____ . C'est combien?   *C'est _____ .*
Voilà.   *Merci. Au revoir.*

notes	à + le = au à + la = à la à + l' = à l' à + les = aux

Part 4 B   I   Les instruments

1   Encercle avec une ligne noire tous les noms au pluriel et écris **des** à côté d'eux.

2   Encercle avec une ligne verte tous les noms au singulier qui commencent par une voyelle ou un 'h muet' et écris **de l'**.

3   Encercle avec une ligne bleue les noms au masculin singulier qui ne commencent pas par une voyelle ou un 'h muet' et écris **du**.

4   Encercle avec une ligne rouge les noms au féminin qui ne commencent pas par une voyelle ou un 'h muet' et écris **de la**.

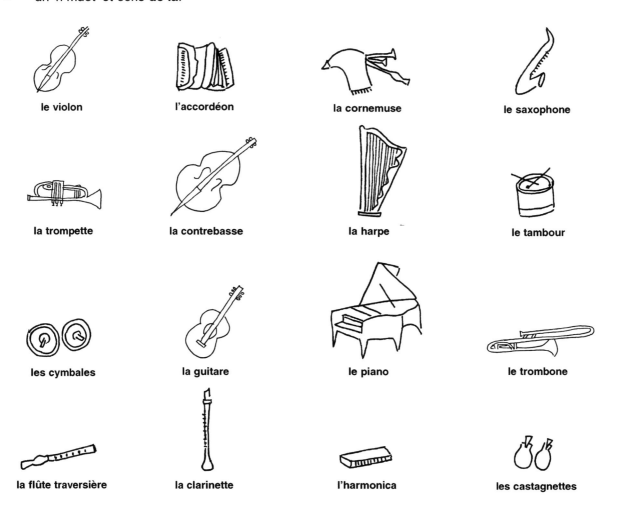

le violon	**l'accordéon**	**la cornemuse**	**le saxophone**
la trompette	**la contrebasse**	**la harpe**	**le tambour**
les cymbales	**la guitare**	**le piano**	**le trombone**
la flûte traversière	**la clarinette**	**l'harmonica**	**les castagnettes**

5   Chaque joueur à son tour mime un instrument. Le professeur demande: 'Il/ elle joue **de** quel instrument?'. La classe réponds 'Il/ elle joue **du/de la/de l'/des** … ' et nomme l'instrument.

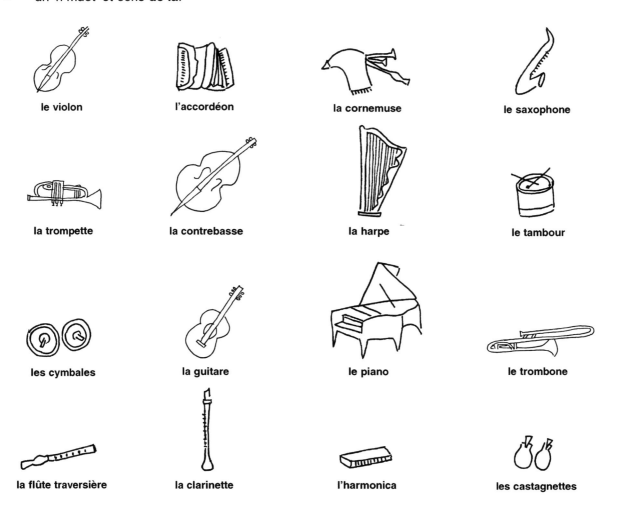

notes	de + le = du de + la = de la de + l' = de l' de + les = des
	Attention! **la** harpe: 'h pas muet' **l'**harmonica: 'h muet'

Getting the basics right © CILT 2001. May be photocopied only within the purchasing institution.

_ _ _ beurre   _ _ _ viande*   _ _ _ poires*   _ _ _ carottes*

_ _ _ baguettes*   _ _ _ chips*   _ _ _ petits pois   _ _ _ jambon

_ _ _ œufs   _ _ _ thé   _ _ _ bananes*   _ _ _ biscuits

_ _ _ café   _ _ _ chocolat   _ _ _ limonade*   _ _ _ glace*

_ _ _ fromage   _ _ _ confiture*   _ _ _ croissants

_ _ _ lait   _ _ _ huile*   _ _ _ jus de fruits   _ _ _ eau minérale*

Attention! * = nom féminin

1 Remplis les blancs avec la bonne préposition (**du, de la, de l'** ou **des**).

2 Relie avec une ligne noire tous les noms au pluriel (**des**).

3 Relie avec une ligne verte tous les noms au singulier qui commencent par une voyelle ou un 'h muet' (**de l'**).

4 Relie avec une ligne bleue les noms au masculin singulier qui ne commencent pas par une voyelle ou un 'h muet' (**du**).

5 Relie avec une ligne rouge les noms au féminin singulier qui ne commencent pas par une voyelle ou un 'h muet' (**de la**).

notes	de + le = du	de + la = de la	de + l' = de l'	de + les = des

86

Les entrées

de la soupe à la tomate	de la soupe au poulet	de la soupe aux légumes
du pâté	du saumon	du caviar
de la salade verte	de la salade de tomates	de la salade niçoise
du melon	du jambon	de l'avocat

Les plats du jour

de la viande	de la dinde	du poulet
du poisson	du canard	de la viande de cheval
du lapin	du steak	du rôti
des hamburgers	des saucisses	de l'omelette

Les légumes

des petits pois	des haricots	des carottes
des pommes de terre	des aubergines	des artichauts
des asperges	du chou-fleur	des champignons
des frites	des oignons	du céleri

Les desserts

du gâteau à la crème	du gâteau au chocolat	du gâteau au café
de la glace à la fraise	de la glace à la vanille	de la glace au chocolat
de la tarte aux pommes	de la tarte aux fraises	de la tarte aux poires
de la crème au chocolat	de la salade de fruits	des fruits

Les boissons

du café	du thé	du chocolat chaud
du coca	de l'orangina	de la limonade
du vin blanc	du vin rouge	de la bière
de l'eau minérale	du jus d'orange	du jus de pommes

Les entrées			
Les plats du jour			
Les légumes			
Les desserts			
Les boissons			

1   En suivant la carte, écris dans la première rangée trois entrées. Dans la deuxième rangée, trois plats du jour. Dans la troisième rangée, trois légumes. Dans la quatrième rangée, trois desserts. Dans la cinquième rangée, trois boissons.

2   Joue au Loto (*Bingo*). Quand tu entends un mot que tu as écrit coche la case vite. Le premier à cocher toutes ses quinze cases gagne!

La carte

Les Entrées

_____
_____
_____

Les Plats du Jour

_____
_____
_____

Les Légumes

_____
_____
_____

Les Desserts

_____
_____
_____

Les Boissons

_____
_____
_____

1 Colorie les plats et les boissons, et puis écris trois entrées, trois plats du jour, trois légumes, trois desserts et trois boissons.

Utilise les prépositions: **du, de la, de l'** et **des.**

1   Commence par écrire le nom des magasins dans les cases:

la boulangerie	le bar	la pharmacie
la charcuterie	l'épicerie	la boucherie
le supermarché	le tabac	la pâtisserie

2   Joue au 'Morpion' avec tes amis. Pour mettre une croix ou un rond dans une case, il faut faire une phrase.

Exemple: J'achète **du** pain et des croissants **à la** boulangerie.

3   Ecris une phrase pour chaque case – dans ton cahier ou sur une autre feuille.

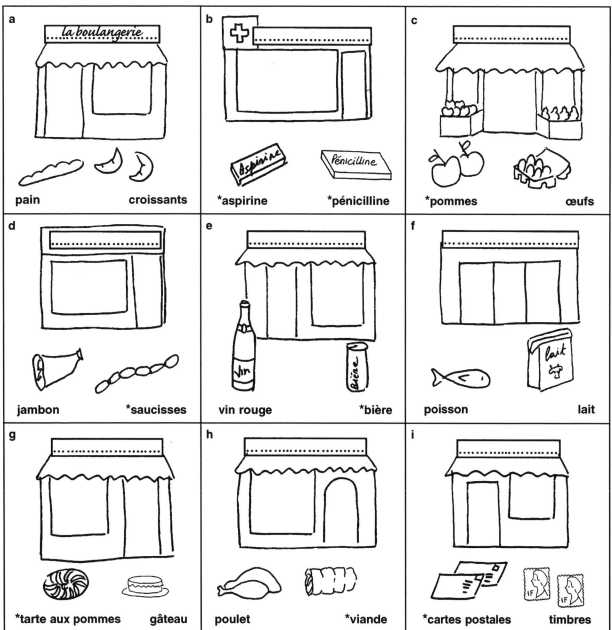

a	b	c
pain croissants	*aspirine *pénicilline	*pommes œufs
d	e	f
jambon *saucisses	vin rouge *bière	poisson lait
g	h	i
*tarte aux pommes gâteau	poulet *viande	*cartes postales timbres

*   **féminin**

Ball games

jouer au ... + masculine noun   **Exemple:** je joue au football

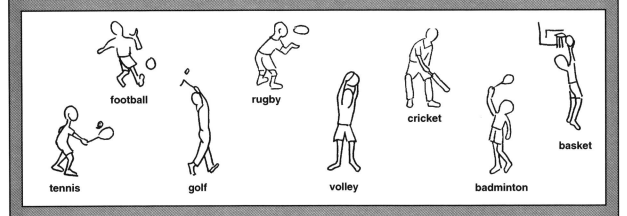

football

rugby

cricket

basket

tennis

golf

volley

badminton

Non-ball games

faire de l'... + noun starting with A, E, I, O or U.   **Exemple:** je fais de l'escrime

escrime   **équitation**   **escalade**

faire du ... + masculine noun starting with a consonant

ski   **judo**   **karaté**   **surf**   **patinage**   **vélo**

faire de la ...   + feminine noun starting with a consonant

voile   **gymnastique**   **natation**

jouer au ...

faire du ...

football gymnastique basket ski

golf natation volley jogging

surf patinage cricket escalade

escrime équitation tennis judo

faire de l'...

faire de la ...

1 **jouer au:** Relie avec une **ligne bleue** les noms masculins des sports que l'on joue avec une balle.

2 **faire de l':** Relie avec une **ligne noire** les noms qui commencent par **a, e, i, o** ou **u** (sports sans balle).

3 **faire de la:** Relie avec une **ligne rouge** les noms féminins qui ne commencent pas par **a, e, i, o** ou **u** (sports sans balle).

4 **faire du:** Relie avec une **ligne verte** les noms masculins qui ne commencent pas par **a, e, i, o** ou **u** (sports sans balle).

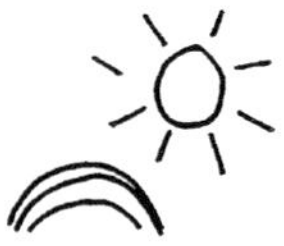 il fait beau	+30 il fait chaud	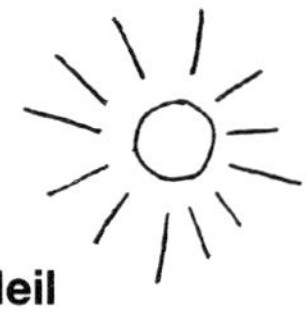 il y a du soleil	-5 il fait froid
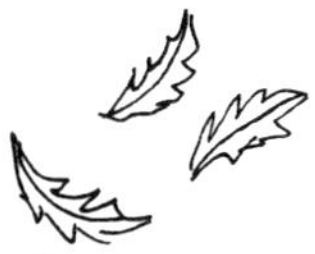 il y a du vent	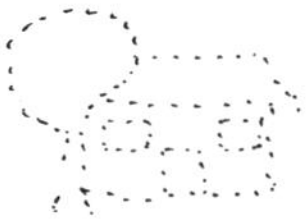 il y a du brouillard	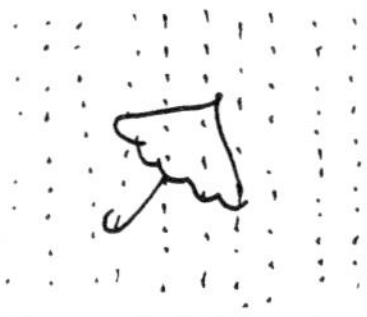 il pleut	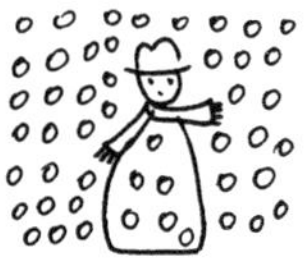 il neige

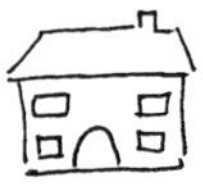 je reste à la maison	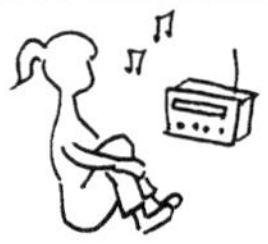 j'écoute la radio	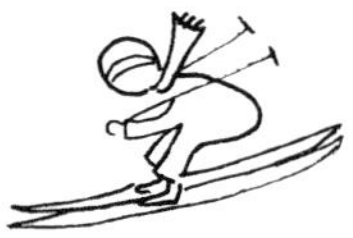 je fais du ski	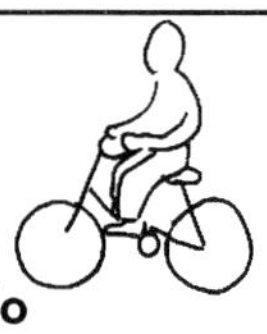 je fais du vélo
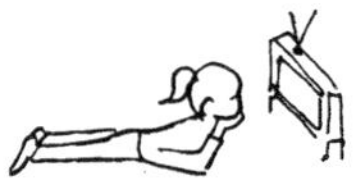 je regarde la télévision	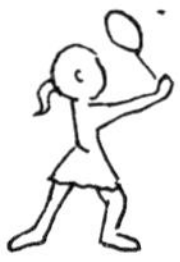 je joue au tennis	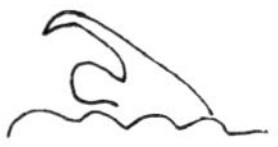 je fais de la natation	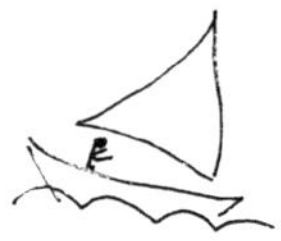 je fais de la voile

1 Suis l'exemple et relie les phrases en utilisant le mot 'quand'.

a   *Quand il fait beau, je joue au tennis.*

b   _____

c   _____

d   _____

e   _____

f   _____

g   _____

h   _____

la bière

l'eau minérale

la limonade

l'orangeade

le thé

le café

le chocolat chaud

le jus de fruit

l'Orangina

le vin rouge

le vin blanc

le lait

1 **Les flashcartes**: prends douze cartes. Sur chaque carte dessine et colorie une boisson différente. Ecris **un** ou **une** et puis nomme la boisson.

2 **Sondage**: Quelle est ta boisson préférée? Demande à tes copains.

Exemple: – Quelle est ta boisson préférée?
  – Je préfère l'Orangina.

3 Complète ces deux listes.

Les boissons chaudes   **Les boissons froides**
Le café

4 Dessine une carte pour un café. Invente un beau nom et décore ta carte. Ensuite fais une liste de toutes les boissons et invente des prix.

Première partie

■ *Maman:* Chaperon Rouge, viens m'aider.

○ *Chaperon Rouge:* Oui, Maman.

■ *Maman:* Ecoute, ta grand-mère est malade. Tu dois aller la voir. Donne-moi ton panier.

○ *Chaperon Rouge:* Voilà, Maman.

■ *Maman:* Regarde, je mets du pain, du beurre, du fromage, du poulet, des tomates, une pomme, une banane, une orange, du raisin, du gâteau, de la confiture et du chocolat. Grand-mère adore le chocolat. Prends ce panier et va vite chez Grand-mère. Ne parle à personne en route. Fais attention! Il y a un méchant loup.

○ *Chaperon Rouge:* Au revoir, Maman.

■ *Maman:* Au revoir, Petit Chaperon Rouge.

Deuxième partie

➤ *Monsieur le Loup:* Bonjour. Qui es-tu? Comment t'appelles-tu?

○ *Chaperon Rouge:* Je m'appelle Petit Chaperon Rouge.

➤ *Monsieur le Loup:* Où vas-tu?

○ *Chaperon Rouge:* Je vais chez ma grand-mère. Elle est malade. Je vais lui donner ce panier. Regarde, il y a du pain, du beurre, du fromage, du poulet, des tomates, une pomme, une banane, une orange, du raisin et du gâteau. Il y a même un pot de confiture et du chocolat!

➤ *Monsieur le Loup:* Où habite ta grand-mère?

○ *Chaperon Rouge:* Voilà, dans cette petite maison, là-bas dans la clairière.

➤ *Monsieur le Loup:* Petit Chaperon Rouge, on fait la course. On va voir qui va arriver le premier. Va par ici, et moi, je vais par là.

○ *Chaperon Rouge:* Oh oui, j'aime ça! Je cours!

Troisième partie

Toc! Toc! Toc!

^ *Grand-mère:* Qui est là?

➤ *Monsieur le Loup:* C'est moi, Petit Chaperon Rouge.

^ *Grand-mère:* Tourne la poignée et la porte s'ouvrira.

➤ *Monsieur le Loup:* Bonjour, Grand-mère.

^ *Grand-mère:* Oh! Mon Dieu! Au secours! Au secours! Aidez-moi! C'est un méchant loup. Oh! j'ai peur. J'ai très peur.

Quatrième partie

Narrateur:	M. Lapin, M. Ecureuil et M. Hérisson rencontrent M. Bûcheron, le père de Chaperon Rouge, dans la forêt.
Le lapin:	Monsieur Bûcheron, Monsieur Bûcheron. Il y a un méchant loup!
▲ *Papa:*	Oh! là! là! là! Mais c'est terrible!
L'écureuil:	Monsieur Bûcheron, Monsieur Bûcheron. Il y a un méchant loup!
	J'ai vu Chaperon Rouge parler au loup!
▲ *Papa:*	Oh! là! là! là! Mais c'est terrible!
Le hérisson:	Monsieur Bûcheron, Monsieur Bûcheron. Il y a un méchant loup!
	J'ai vu Chaperon Rouge parler au loup!
	J'ai vu le loup entrer chez Grand-mère!
▲ *Papa:*	Oh! là! là! là! Mais c'est terrible! Allons! Vite! Vite! Vite!

Cinquième partie

Narrateur:	Le méchant loup attaque la pauvre grand-mère, lui tire sa chemise de nuit, son bonnet, ses lunettes et quand il entend Petit Chaperon Rouge taper à la porte, il cache grand-mère dans l'armoire. Il met vite la chemise de nuit, le bonnet et les lunettes et se couche au lit. Petit Chaperon Rouge tape à la porte. Toc! Toc! Toc!
➤ *Monsieur le Loup:*	Qui est là?
○ *Chaperon Rouge:*	C'est moi. Petit Chaperon Rouge!
➤ *Monsieur le Loup:*	Tourne la poignée et la porte s'ouvrira.
Narrateur:	Petit Chaperon Rouge entre dans la chambre. Elle regarde sa grand-mère. Elle est étonnée. Elle se frotte les yeux.

○ *Chaperon Rouge:*	Grand-mère, que tu as de grands yeux!
➤ *Monsieur le Loup:*	C'est pour mieux te voir, mon enfant!
○ *Chaperon Rouge:*	Grand-mère, que tu as un grand nez!
➤ *Monsieur le Loup:*	C'est pour mieux te sentir, mon enfant!
○ *Chaperon Rouge:*	Grand-mère, que tu as de grandes oreilles!
➤ *Monsieur le Loup:*	C'est pour mieux t'entendre, mon enfant!
○ *Chaperon Rouge:*	Grand-mère, que tu as une grande bouche et de grandes dents!
➤ *Monsieur le Loup:*	C'est pour mieux te manger, mon enfant!
○ *Chaperon Rouge:*	Au secours! Au secours! Aidez-moi. Au loup! Au loup!
Narrateur:	Le méchant loup saute sur Petit Chaperon Rouge. Il ouvre sa grande bouche, mais à ce moment le père de Chaperon Rouge arrive. Il saute sur le loup et avec son couteau il tape le loup. Le loup sort du lit. Il s'échappe par la fenêtre. Chaperon Rouge se jette dans les bras de son père.

○ *Chaperon Rouge:*   Papa! Papa! Papa! Merci, Papa!

Narrateur: Chaperon Rouge pleure.

▲ *Papa:*   Où est Grand-mère?

○ *Chaperon Rouge:*   Je ne sais pas.

^ *Grand-mère:*   Au secours! Au secours! Je suis dans l'armoire! Aidez-moi. Je veux sortir! Au secours!

▲ *Papa:*   Grand-Mère, où es-tu?

^ *Grand-mère:*   Dans l'armoire. Ouvre vite! J'étouffe!

▲ *Papa:*   Voilà! J'ouvre l'armoire.

Narrateur: Chaperon Rouge et Papa embrassent Grand-mère.

○ *Chaperon Rouge:*   Pardon! Pardon!

▲ *Papa:*   Ça va, grand-mère? Tu as mal?

^ *Grand-mère:*   Je vais bien, merci. Et toi, Petit Chaperon Rouge? Ça va?

○ *Chaperon Rouge:*   Oui, ça va bien merci.

▲ *Papa:*   Cesse de pleurer, Chaperon Rouge. Rappelle toi: 'Il ne faut jamais parler aux gens, que tu ne connais pas'.

References

Biriotti L, Young Pathfinder 8: *Grammar is fun* (CILT, 1999)

Kay J, *Un kilo de chansons* (Mary Glasgow Publications, 1978). Cassette, lyrics and teacher's notes

Scibor T, *Zozo's French party* (Club Tricolore, 1993). Cassette. (Supplier of teaching resources for French, German, Spanish and Italian. Tel: 020 7924 4649.)

Skarbek C, Young Pathfinder 5: *First steps to reading and writing* (CILT, 1998)